dedication

This book is dedicated to YOU!

*Within these pages we will explore the mysteries, mistakes, and magic of faux finishing and reveal that Wall Wizards aren't magical, but just people with a lot of "tricks up their sleeves." Now that you have my secrets, don't be afraid to use them. It is my hope they will serve you well. Every time you apply them, you prove Dorothy was right: there really is **no place like home!***

Thank-yous

It takes a village to raise a "Wizard." My special thanks:

To my mom, for her artistic influence. To my dad, for his work ethic. To my grandfather, for instilling me with the power of "why."

To the Meredith Corporation, especially Ken, Dan, and Doug, for their belief in the "magic" of the Wizard.

To my children, Paul, Scott, and Kelli, whom I love, and who are the future.

And most of all, to my wife and partner, Virginia, who shares all my dreams. Thank you for all your love and support throughout our journeys together.

Table of contents

faux finish SECRETS

from **Brian Santos**
The Wall Wizard

Meredith® Books
Des Moines, Iowa

Faux Finish Secrets from Brian Santos, The Wall Wizard
Editor: Ken Sidey
Contributing Writer: Dan Weeks
Graphic Designers: Chris Conyers, Jana Rogness, Beth Runcie,
    Joe Wysong (Conyers Design, Inc.)
Copy Chief: Terri Fredrickson
Publishing Operations Manager: Karen Schirm
Senior Editor, Asset and Information Manager: Phillip Morgan
Edit and Design Production Coordinator: Mary Lee Gavin
Editorial and Design Assistant: Renee E. McAtee
Book Production Managers: Pam Kvitne,
    Marjorie J. Schenkelberg, Rick von Holdt, Mark Weaver
Contributing Copy Editor: Stacey Schildroth
Contributing Proofreaders: Janet Anderson, Joel Marvin,
    Cheri Madison, Paula Reece
Illustrator: Michael Burns
Photographers: Doug Hetherington, Scott Little
Indexer: Donald Glassman
Editorial and Design Assistant: Renee E. McAtee

Meredith® Books
Executive Director, Editorial: Gregory H. Kayko
Executive Director, Design: Matt Strelecki
Managing Editor: Amy Tincher-Durik
Executive Editor/Group Manager: Benjamin W. Allen
Senior Associate Design Director: Doug Samuelson
Marketing Product Manager: Isaac Petersen

Publisher and Editor in Chief: James D. Blume
Editorial Director: Linda Raglan Cunningham
Executive Director, New Business Development: Todd M. Davis
Executive Director, Sales: Ken Zagor
Director, Operations: George A. Susral
Director, Production: Douglas M. Johnston
Director, Marketing: Amy Nichols
Business Director: Jim Leonard

Vice President and General Manager: Douglas J. Guendel

Meredith Publishing Group
President: Jack Griffin
Executive Vice President: Bob Mate

Meredith Corporation
Chairman and Chief Executive Officer: William T. Kerr
President and Chief Operating Officer: Stephen M. Lacy

In Memoriam: E. T. Meredith III (1933-2003)

All of us at Meredith® Books are dedicated to providing you
with the information and ideas you need to enhance your home
and garden. We welcome your comments and suggestions.
Write to us at:
Meredith Books
Home Improvement Books Department
1716 Locust St.
Des Moines, IA 50309-3023

NOTE TO THE READERS: Due to differing conditions, tools, and individual skills, Meredith Corporation assumes no responsibility for any damages, injuries suffered, or losses incurred as a result of following the information published in this book. Before beginning any project, review the instructions carefully, and if any doubts or questions remain, consult local experts or authorities. Because codes and regulations vary greatly, you always should check with authorities to ensure that your project complies with all applicable local codes and regulations. Always read and observe all of the safety precautions provided by manufacturers of any tools, equipment, or supplies, and follow all accepted safety procedures.

chapter 1

introduction

"That's so cool! How do you do that?" is an exclamation I hear all the time as I demonstrate faux finishes, such as rag-rolling, graining, marbling, strié, and many more, in my workshops at home shows around the world. The question that inevitably follows my demonstration is "Can I do that?"

My answer: Sure! With the proper understanding of how to achieve each finish, almost anyone can create beautiful faux effects. And once you know and master these basics, you can use your imagination to create a variety of results.

Meet the Wizard

As a fourth-generation painting contractor and faux finisher, my philosophy is simple: Knowledge is power. The magic is in you!

One obstacle lies between you and all the wonder of faux finishing: fear. You're going to make a few mistakes, but what are you really risking? A can of paint! So go ahead, dive in and try. I'll be with you every step of the way.

First, you'll learn what a faux effect is and which effect to use where. Each faux technique produces certain results: Some, such as sponging or textured plaster, make for great backgrounds. Others, such as marble or wood grains, create focal points. Some effects work better with one type of architecture than another. So before you learn how to faux finish, you need to learn how to "read" a room and decide which finish to use. That's why we'll start with a "Faux Showcase" in Chapter 2. In it we'll take a tour of some wonderful examples of great faux finishes. I'll help you look at the rooms through a professional's eyes, explaining how each finish works with the room's architecture, furnishings, and accessories to create its look, mood, and feel.

Second, you'll learn how to apply paint neatly and efficiently. That's why the middle chapters of this book are devoted to techniques that will turn painting from a hair-pulling, stressful mess to a smooth, efficient process that creates great results. WIthin this book are dozens of tips on tools, techniques, and materials that many professional painters don't even know about, but that you can master easily and effectively.

Finally, in the last chapter, you'll learn how specific faux effects are achieved. More than that, I'll help you understand the "why" behind the "how-to"—which is something most other books, classes, and workshops on faux finishing never tell you! How can you know what to do if you don't understand why you're doing it? I'll reveal the science behind the art so you can create your own wall magic.

What are you
really risking?
A can of paint!
So go ahead,
dive in and try!

You'll learn the principles all faux finishers use to create the illusion of depth and dimension, highlight and shadow, texture and grain begin with a few basic insights about light and perception. You'll become aware of the basic tools and techniques needed to apply these insights and create gorgeous effects.

By the time you finish this book, you'll have all the information you need to produce finishes that convincingly imitate granite, marble, exotic woods, and even puffy white clouds.

Discover how to create these effects by trial and error, experimentation and failure—but with no fear! In my 25 years of faux finishing, I've made every kind of mistake you can think of and some you can't even imagine! I've created a few simple tips and tricks that will help your project go smoothly.

All you need are a few basic materials, a little common sense, and a bit of patience.

Welcome to the Wizard's Workshop!

Let's get started!

chapter 2
faux showcase

Welcome to the gallery of effects! In this chapter you'll discover some beautiful examples of finishes you can achieve with the help of this book. More importantly you'll learn you *HOW* each effect works to bring out the best in the room in which it is featured, as well as *WHERE, WHEN,* and *WHY* you might want to use the same effect in your own home. Finally I'll point out *WHERE TO TURN* in this book for step-by-step information on how to create a similar finish.

combed out

Combing can add visual texture, color play, and either an offset freshness or a rhythmic symmetry to a surface depending on how it is applied. It can also mimic or suggest other materials, such as wallpaper, fabric, or grass cloth. Traditionally a vertical effect, it seems to add visual height to a room. Unlike precisely painted stripes or machine-printed wallpaper, however, it has the subtle imperfections of handcraftsmanship and generates interest and character on otherwise plain walls.

Mixed marriage

A fusion of French and Asian influences, the bath above uses a combed moiré pattern on the walls. This weaving finish creates an interference pattern similar to that seen on fabrics by superimposing wavy lines on straight ones. The effect also adds a visual luster to the room. To complete the room, the organic Asian influences, seen in the drapery and window screen, paintings, grass mat, and sandals, unite with the French-inspired cording at the intersection of the wall and ceiling planes and the graceful curves of the metal towel stand.

 For more information on combing techniques, see page 106.

Deft detail

This close-up view of another area of the room, pictured on the opposite page, shows how careful attention to scale can really pay off when executing a faux finish: the combed stripes in the upper wall section are just thick enough to appear to be grasslike complements to the leaves on the lampshade. And the sponge finish mimics—in scale as well as color—the textured cork bulletin boards.

Attractive opposites

Above is a great example of using multiple faux effects with opposing characteristics in a single space. Combing is dominant here, both in the treatment above the wainscot molding and, in reversed colors, on the drawers of the repurposed chest. The rhythmic lines of the combed upper wall section work well with the abstract asymmetry of a sponge-painted lower wall—an area that also offers a contrast in color. Opposites help balance this composition: brushed metal on the pitcher and drawer pull contrasts with the organic elements such as the leaf-wrapped candles and cascading spider plant. Plain paint alone can create contrast, but it lacks the personality and variety that faux finishes have—characteristics that allow control of the subtleties of depth, texture, rhythm, and scale that make a setting such as this one so pleasing to the eye.

For more information on combing techniques, see page 106.

why not a **wash?**

Washes color a surface but are translucent, allowing the background color to show through. They're a good choice when you want to give tone and highlight the character of the underlying wall, and impart softness.

Block wash

This technique, called "block wash," creates a finish with a subtle, softly mottled look. It is a more contemporary looking, abstract effect than the more traditional wash finish. This finish is created by painting randomly distributed blocks of color on the wall, then mixing, blending, and overlapping them. It's an ideal wall effect for this entryway, where traditional architecture plays off modern geometric shapes and accessories: a contemporary interpretation of a traditional table topped with a minimalist sculpture and a simple flower arrangement.

 For more information on how to create a color wash finish, see page 114.

Cartoon primitive

Color washes can also convey a visual texture of their own to a simple painted wall. That's what's going on here: the wash was applied in swirling strokes that form an animated, bubbly look, complementing the print on the tablecloth and the balloon-like curves of the overstuffed furniture. Combined with the exuberant, inviting pattern on the seating pieces' pillows and slipcovers, the finish gives the room a playful quality. A low, solid-looking coffee table, heavy bowl, and sisal rug ground the space with their visual weight, organic materials, and earthy tones. In this case, the room's balance doesn't come from the formal symmetry, but from the pleasing tension between opposing shapes, textures, and materials.

rag on!

Bold bath

This powder room gets its form and function from a balance of graphic, hard-edged geometry and a soft, swirling faux effect that provides a rich, colorful, complementary background. The crisp, linear shapes of the room's framed artwork, moldings, shelving—even the tilework—seem to float in front of the wall's backdrop. The result makes this small room seem larger, softer, and airier than it might if painted a plain color. To prevent this accessory-filled space from seeming cluttered, the walls take their color from the tile and contrast nicely with the white accents.

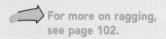
For more on ragging, see page 102.

Sublime and subtle

A pale yellow glaze showcases rich textiles and antique furniture, right. The wall's yellow tinge gives the dark walnut chest a warm, rich look and causes the braided cord on the arm of the chair to leap to the foreground.

For more info on highlight and shadow, see page 42.

Ragging is a technique for giving a subtle, random, softly mottled look to a wall. It adds a warmth and organic feel to a room and offers a great contrast to crisp, graphic room details. Ragging's tonal color values also harmonize objects of different colors and intensities in a way that a plain, solid-color wall cannot.

Revisionist retro

The reproduction bath below has all the hallmarks of antiquity—vintage-style lighting, nickel-plated fixtures, running-bond tile, and furniture-style vanity sink bases. But there's a welcome twist: a wash of fluid color on the walls above the tile wainscot prevents the room from feeling too rigid and antiseptic, nicely updating the vintage look. Here the technique adds fluidity and softness to a room with strong, crisp architecture.

the richness of ragging

Turkish deco

Because faux effects can be multi-hued and complex rather than homogeneous and uniform, the finishes are ideal hosts for elements from diverse styles, ages, and even cultures. If you're looking for an eclectic mix, ask yourself what combination of colors, tones, and values might pull together all the pieces of your room. Above, Middle Eastern details—a carved column, hammered-metal vase, ornamental metal drapery rods, and handmade rug—play a duet with a clean-lined, deco-style chaise and table. A ragged wall picks up colors from both stylistic elements, emphasizing their harmony even as they celebrate their differences.

 For more information about determining how a particular effect will look in a specific room, see page 163.

Modern metallic

Say "faux finish" and most people think "old world" or "traditional." But faux finishes aren't confined to any one style or era, as the modern bath, left, proves. This room is filled with contemporary hallmarks: overscale geometric shapes, conspicuous use of metals, and lots of highly polished surfaces. Fluid elements help add balance and soften the room's contemporary look. A ragged finish on the wall combines a random, organic pattern and texture with a metallic tone. Along with the concrete vase on the vanity top and the wooden vanity support, the faux finish gives a reassuring, grounded feel to a room that might otherwise appear completely synthetic, antiseptic, and shiney.

Country colonial

This room in a vintage East-Coast house, right, combines an almost puritanical spareness with welcoming, overstuffed comfort and sense of stability. The furniture and pillows, colorfully patterned fabrics, and touch of ruffle and fringe help warm and soften the architecture's plain moldings and plank floors. The rag finish on the wall mediates between these two extremes. Its buttery yellow tone mimics the sunshine streaming through the 12-over-12 window, while the soft mottled appearance blends with the room's fabrics and hints at aged plaster.

For more information on applying texture to surfaces, see pages 125 and 164.

give it a **rustic** feel

Sepia showcase

The rustic finish on the wall behind the elegant little collection of old family photos and memorabilia, below, provides an appropriate setting for viewing these historic items. The yellowed mat of the large print visually bleeds into the wall around it, making it look almost rooted to the spot. Yet the random, mottled wall tone is light enough to contrast nicely with the strong shapes and various colors of the frame, lamp, and furniture.

Barn again

This home, above, newly built in the style of an antique barn converted to living quarters, is all about texture and the patina of age. The weathered door, country antiques, and plaster-and-rafter ceiling speak of a building that proudly wears the marks of long use. The new walls have been distressed with a two-tone finish that suggests swirling trowel marks and the irregular yellowing of an antique paint job.

Elemental elegance

This monochromatic modern bath, right, emphasizes texture rather than color. It also reverses expectations: the fabric drape is shiny and metallic while the walls have a coarse texture and a blotchy boldness that breaks up the hard-edged architecture.

Rustic finishes visually age new surfaces and give them an organic character. The technique can be used to harmonize new architecture with antique furnishings or memorabilia, or to create an organic feel to a modern space.

 For more information on rustic finishes, see page 122.

 For more information on how to prepare walls for the application of a faux finish, see page 64.

Texture can add interest and dimension to a wall surface. Depending on how it's applied, texture can be coarse or smooth, consistent in tone or variegated, highly dimensional in appearance or relatively shallow, rough to the touch or smooth.

Formal complements

Filled with delicate china, crystal, marquetry inlay, and pristine white moldings, the formal living room, opposite, gains warmth and approachability from a textured wall finish. The visually textured walls give the illusion of a fabric backdrop for the glossy wood, stone, glass, and metal objects on display, and offer a supporting contrast to the crisp white moldings and Venetian blinds.

Cozy French country

The walls of the breakfast nook, right, were rubbed with a mixture of glaze and plaster to create a surface that's textural both to the eye and to the touch. The treatment is an easy way to imitate the rough-plastered walls found in French provincial farmhouses. As with almost any faux finish, you can apply it right over properly prepared drywall. Aged wrought metal furnishings and a chandelier complete the look.

Kind of a drag

The vertical dragging motion that created the finish at right respects the lines of the simple, elegant picture frame and inlaid bird's-eye maple buffet. Neither as formal as the dining room, opposite, nor as informal as the breakfast nook above, this wall uses a texture midway between the two in refinement: the strié exhibits some deliberate irregularities in tone that highlight its handcraftsmanship.

 For more information on dragging techniques, see page 129.

say it with stripes

Stripes can be plain or fancy, formal or informal, highly graphic or subtly tone-on-tone. How they're executed depends on the particular result you're after, but in general, stripes make a room appear taller and add character to otherwise blank walls.

Tone on tone

The same basic technique creates an entirely different look at right. Here the stripes are asymmetrical—of different widths. And they're tone-on-tone—two subtle variations of the same color, rather than contrasting colors. But as in the formal living room, the effect complements other elements in the room. The playfully random widths of the stripes, for example, repeat the irregular rhythms of the folds in the drapery, the tassels on the bed's throw, and the slightly uneven weave of the textured carpet. The blue contrasts nicely with the earthy tones of the textiles and pickled birch floor, symbolically adding an element of sky or water to the room.

 To create stripes, see page 126. For strié, see page 129.

Stripes on stripes

In the formal living room, opposite, stripes combine with a strié—a combing technique—to create a lively effect that works well with the room's traditional architecture. The stripes' regular dimension gives a soothing rhythm to the room; the strié softens the color contrast, preventing the result from appearing too jarring. The effect was executed with care to respect the room's architectural elements and proportions too. For instance, the pattern lines up exactly with the edge of the fireplace surround and subtly echoes both the dentil molding under the mantelpiece and the flutes in the columns that frame the hearth. The result adds richness and detail, yet harmonizes beautifully with the room's existing structure and ornament.

 For more information on the use of color see page 36.

strike up the bands

Think horizontal

Big, bold bands of intense tangerine and pumpkin colors, above, unify an eclectic decorating scheme. The chairs are vaguely Edwardian in style, the table has deco lines, the artwork is definitely abstract, the lamp is contemporary, and the oversized baseboard moldings are Victorian. The bands pull all these elements together by repeating the colors in the upholstery and the artwork, and mimicking the broad horizontal line of the room's oversized baseboard molding. Without the regular swaths of horizontal color, the bold art might seem a bit disorienting, but the bands provide a stable "horizon" and a sense of predictable regularity that balances the art's abstract composition. The intense colors also allow the plain white lampshade, table, and chair pillows to create their own abstract composition against the two-tone wall.

 For more about proportion, see page 129.

Horizontal bands make a room seem longer, wider, and less lofty. They're great for small rooms with high ceilings, visually restoring the space to more pleasing proportions. Bands also create a horizon line, causing your eye to sweep around the room—useful if the space has no windows or other natural focal point.

Echo with accessories

In addition to giving a room its overall character, this faux finish also showcases accessories and details. Here stacked towels echo the wall's color scheme and pattern. Even the shadow-box-like geometry of the drawerless chest, repurposed as a display and storage case, has linear proportions inspired by the wall treatment. On top of the chest, an orderly collection of vintage bottles, each holding a tulip, adds dimension and draws the eye to the abstract painting on the wall.

For accent colors, see page 41.

The anti-focal point

In this railroad-themed bedroom, graphic shapes and high contrast are everywhere. The cream and beige bands create a sense of unity, drawing your gaze across the entire room instead of fixing on a main focal point. The cream color warms up the space, preparing the eye for the bright red accents splashed throughout the room. The horizontal lines play on the railroad-track theme. Thanks to the background, the room is neither cartoonish nor cutesy but a sophisticated interpretation of a childhood fascination with trains and travel.

For information on masking, see page 69.

dare to do diamonds

Tone on tone

Any geometric pattern creates a highly structured rhythm, but that doesn't mean it has to be overwhelming. By toning down the contrast between the shapes to no more than a shade or two of difference, the effect on the wall below creates a backdrop for a stone fireplace. The interplay strikes a nice balance: the diamonds' colors complement those in the rock while the shapes contrast with the masonry's horizontal lines.

For information on how to create a diamond effect, see page 160.

Pattern on pattern

An under-the-eaves attic bedroom in a rustic cabin uses a diamond-painted floor to stretch its dimensions both inside and outside the room. The repeating pattern on the floor echoes the repeating doors, a hall-of-mirrors illusion that gives the entire upper story a sense of infinite length. Back in the bedroom, the diamonds playfully interact with the room's other elements: the slanted roofline, the board walls, the dark paneled doors and moldings and the geometric quilts. The interplay between the quilts and the floor is deft: By varying the scale of the patterns, but keeping the tone and the values similar, the two bedcoverings and the floor complement rather than compete with one another.

 For information about sizing diamonds to a surface, see page 160.

Diamonds combine color and shape to create a pattern that can be a bold focal point or a subtle backdrop. It all depends on the colors, scale, and degree of contrast you employ. These squares-turned-on-edge can be used to add energy to bland spaces. Applied to a floor, diamonds make a room feel larger, guiding your eye down the points that visually stretch across the room.

build some blocks

Blocks bring to mind a regular array, such as a brick wall built of virtually identical units. Paint, however, allows a much greater freedom of color, scale, and arrangement. Explore the possibilities!

It's hip to be square

The treatment on the living room wall, left, took its dimensional cue from the blocky-looking chairs in the foreground. Flat white "muntins" between the variegated yellow and rose blocks create the impression of a sunny morning viewed through the panes of an overscaled wall of windows, adding warmth, cheer, and an abstract "view" to this cozy corner.

Upscale blocks

Multicolored, small-scale tile on the vanity and mirror surround in the bathroom, right, inspired the colors and shape of the faux finish in this room. The element of contrast here is scale: the faux finished wall blows up the tiles' grid of squares to grand proportions. The result is an expansive quilt of pastel blocks and a restful backdrop for the pixilated tiled surfaces. Stacked and hanging towels and a blonde wood bench pull from the same palette, bringing colors off the walls and into the room.

For more information on how to create block effects, see page 130.

back to nature

Reach for the sky

Clouds are a great way to expand a room's visual space in a way that gives the imagination room to soar. They're particularly effective when supporting a theme—often a transportation theme, as they suggest distant horizons and faraway places. This young boy's room is a great example: clouds on the wall and the ceiling recede into infinity. A chair rail, however, offers a definite horizon that prevents a viewer from feeling disoriented. Beneath the rail, a travel-themed wallcovering in earth tones furthers the theme while visually grounding the room. Planes, trains, and autos on a wallcovering border, window valances, and accessories tie the look together.

For more information on painting cloud effects, see page 140.

Faux effects are nearly limitless in their variety and application. In addition to those traditional effects presented on the preceeding pages, here are a few other, more advanced techniques you may want to try. They take some practice, procedure, and patience, but the results are stunning!

Simply marbleous

Marble is a premium material that implies the ultimate in luxury. Here it's applied to the walls as a paint treatment in an elegant bathroom. Usually, applying such a rich technique to so much wall space would be overwhelming. This room is the exception to the rule: the antique furnishings, accessories, Oriental carpet, and gold-plated tub fixtures make a strong statement of elegance, and the marble supports it nicely. The effect's gold and brown veins complement the hues of the furnishings and floors, while the white background offers a welcome tonal contrast. One of the tricks of creating a convincing effect is to reproduce the look of a real chunk of stone—and to know how real marble is hung.

 For more information on marbling techniques, see page 152.

You wood if you could

Woodgrained finishes offer another way to convincingly imitate nature—in this case by "paneling" an entryway in pickled oak. Again, such a dramatic effect is often used sparingly—perhaps on one wall only, on a wainscot, or on woodwork as a focal point. Here, however, the home's strong, traditional architecture, abundant artwork, and a character-rich sideboard prevent the effect from stealing the show. It "fits" here, because wood paneling similar to this might have been used on a house of this style and period.

 For more information on wood grain techniques, see page 146.

chapter 3

contrast
and color

Faux finishing is all about creating
a three-dimensional look on a two-
dimensional surface. Walls have height
and width, but they're flat surfaces and
have no depth. A faux finish gives the
wall the illusion of depth—the sense
that you're not looking at the wall, but
that you're looking *into* the surface.

At first, the idea of creating a three-dimensional look on a two-dimensional wall using nothing more than paint and glaze might sound a little strange. After all, faux finishes imitate natural materials, such as wood, stone, and leather, that are flat.

Well, they're not actually flat. Leather, of course, has a surface texture. Stone, such as granite or marble, has a crystalline structure. Some of the minerals that make up the crystals are clear or translucent, so you actually look into the stone, sometimes only for microscopic distances, and sometimes, in the case of a largely translucent stone such as quartz, for quite a distance. Wood grain is similar. Some woods have grain that's so translucent it conducts light fiberoptically, causing the wood to shimmer and flash in direct light, giving it a gemlike quality.

Faux finishes recreate these natural surfaces in the same two ways. When we're applying a faux finish, we create *actual depth* by using a glaze—a semitransparent finish that allows us to see through the glaze layer and into the color of the paint underneath. The distance we see into the finish through the glaze is only the microscopic thickness of the glaze coat itself. But like the tiny quartz crystal embedded in a granite slab or the translucent wood fiber as thick as a human hair, that distance is enough to impart a sense of depth to the surface. I'll talk more about glazes later in the book.

As faux finishers, we control *apparent depth.* That's because apparent depth is the degree of contrast between a material's highlights and its shadows. Faux finishing always involves using at least two colors—a highlight color and a shadow color. The degree of contrast between these colors determines the apparent depth of the finish.

Often we use a darker-colored glaze over a lighter-colored base coat, but sometimes we reverse the situation and use a lighter-colored glaze over a darker-colored base coat. It all depends on the nature of the effect you want to create.

So there you have it: The magic of faux finishing is in fooling your eye with the illusion of highlights and shadows.

Instead of looking at two different colors of paint on a flat wall, the eye thinks it sees a rich, textured surface with depth.

There's even more! What colors you choose to combine, and the tools and techniques you use to apply them determine whether the resulting surface looks like stone, a skyscape, fine wood paneling, textured plaster, or thousands of other finishes. The art and craft of faux finishing can take a lifetime to explore. Even after 25 years, I'm still learning and creating new techniques, finding and using new tools (or often, common tools in uncommon ways), and experimenting and discovering new results.

But they all use the same principle—the contrast between highlight and shadow—to bring off their particular look. Keep this in mind as you read about and practice the techniques I share with you.

While contrast plays an important role with faux effects, you also need a basic understanding of color. That *doesn't* mean you must be an artist—not at all. The relationships of colors to one another, and to other colors in the same family, is not an art. It's a science. In its simplest terms, it's easy to comprehend. After reading the next few pages, you'll have the knowledge and understanding of color as it applies to faux finishing. ●

Is this faux real? I'm holding the genuine piece of marble, which I used as a guide to create the faux finish on the wall panel behind it.

Color variations

All colors have three characteristics: hue, intensity, and value. These variations result in an endless range of colors.

HUE

Hue is the purest form of a color.

INTENSITY

Intensity describes a color's degree of purity, or saturation. Saturated colors appear more vivid to the eye. You can diminish the intensity of a color by adding either white or black to it; the color becomes paler or grayer depending on how much you add.

VALUE

Value refers to the relative lightness or darkness of a color. As a color is mixed with white, gray, or black, it moves away from its pure color, becoming a tint, shade, or tone.

TINT is a color that has been lightened by the addition of white. The more white you add, the paler the color. For example, pinks are tints of pure red. On the color wheel, tints lie inside the pure hues and move toward the center of the wheel as they get progressively lighter.

SHADE is a color that has been darkened by the addition of black. The more black you add, the darker the color. Forest green is a shade of pure green. Shades lie outside the pure colors on the color wheel and move outward as they get darker.

The vivid blue above combines with the pale yellow of the walls to display a classic mix of intensities. The colors below all come on strong, from the cabinet fronts to the walls to the border around the mirror.

TONE is a color that has been modified with gray, creating a more subtle or toned-down version of a color. Mustard is a tone of yellow.

NEUTRAL COLORS

Neutral colors are white, black, and gray, which are blends of white and black. Technically white and black are noncolors because white reflects all the colors in the full visible spectrum, and black absorbs all of them. Working with different values of colors in your decorating plan is more pleasing than choosing colors of the same value; it keeps colors from competing with one another. ●

The effect of low-value color selections, such as the peach bed ruffle, tablecloth, and pillows, is to create a quiet atmosphere, perfect for a bedroom.

Shades

VALUE

Tints

| Black | 25% Hue 75% Black | 50% Hue 50% Black | 75% Hue 25% Black | Hue | 75% Hue 25% White | 50% Hue 50% White | 25% Hue 75% White | White |

75% Color 25% Gray

50% Color 50% Gray

25% Color 75% Gray

Gray

TONE

color value scale

A color value scale is a handy tool when creating faux finishes. The value scale is separated into bars ranging from black at one end to white at the other, with the hue (pure color) in the middle. The shades or tints represent the relative darkness or lightness of a color (usually shown as 10 values for convenience on the scale, although the actual range of colors is continuous). Adding or subtracting black or white to the hue controls the value. The value scale shows the effect of adding a neutral gray ("gray-dation") to the tints and shades.

Color and light

Color comes to your eyes as reflected light. Change the type of light, and you will change the color. You need to control light sources, as well as the paint on a wall, to control color. Here are four types of light that affect color:

NATURAL LIGHT

Natural light is sunlight (top photo), the purest light and the easiest on the eye. It covers the entire spectrum of light and shows the truest color.

GENERAL LIGHTING

General light is also known as ambient lighting. This artificial light can come from incandescent, fluorescent, or halogen sources. "Daylight" bulbs provide a broader spectrum of light than standard bulbs, producing a warmer, more natural effect.

TASK LIGHTING

Task lighting highlights a work space or feature area. Track lighting and undercabinet lighting are examples of this type of light.

ACCENT OR SPECIALTY LIGHTING

Accent lighting (bottom photo) adds visual interest and drama to your decor. Lamps are common examples of accent lighting. ●

color test

Before you start applying your choice of faux finish to a wall, create it on a piece of white 24×30-inch foam-core board. When it's dry, move the board around the room, testing the finish in a variety of light conditions. Hold it vertically on the walls to view it. This method also lets you see how furniture and accessories in a room look when positioned against or next to a particular finish.

The right amount of color

Getting the right amount of color in a room is the most important part of a color plan. It's also the most difficult. In fact, few people feel confident creating a color plan, so they tend to use a favorite color over and over until it loses its impact. Avoid this common mistake by using one of the following methods to create your color plan.

ONE DOMINANT COLOR

Use one color in its different values and intensities over most of the room, then add its complementary colors as accents on smaller furniture pieces, window coverings, accent rugs, and accessories such as pillows. A monochromatic arrangement is another version of this design plan. It uses one color in shades and tints of different values and adds one accent color. The accent color is a contrast of the base color—often its complement.

SPLIT COLORS

This plan requires significant contrast in the values and intensities of colors to be effective. For example, use one color on the walls, the window coverings, and most upholstered furniture. Choose a different color for the floor, and add a third color and variations of the first two for accent furniture and accessories.

TWO DOMINANT COLORS

For this color plan, select one dominant color for the walls, floor, and smaller pieces of furniture and another color for the major pieces of furniture. Because you are working with only two colors, pay special attention to the mix of contrasting values and intensities. Also add texture contrast in the paint or wallcovering or in the upholstery and accessory fabrics. ●

Blue dominates the room, above top, appearing not only on the walls but also in the glassware and pitcher, on the bowl, and even on the ceramic chicken. The doors in the kitchen, above middle, feature a lighter value color, while the casework provides a darker but complementary color. The living room walls, above, are painted with one strong color; the fireplace offers a second, equally strong selection.

controlling contrast

Applying a dark glaze over a light base coat results in a rich, dramatic look. Why? Because most home interiors are light colored, so adding dark creates a stark contrast. A dark element in most rooms draws the eye to it like a magnet.

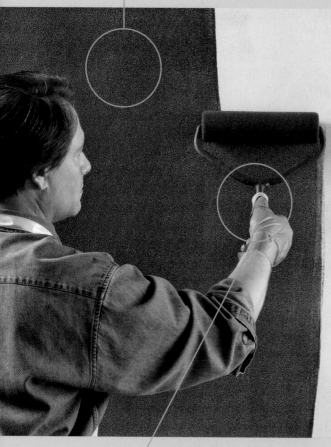

Here's what it looks like when you roll a black glaze onto a white wall. Glaze isn't the same as paint—the pigments are diluted in a clear medium, resulting in a translucent finish. When glaze is rolled on evenly, it's all the same thickness, so the entire glazed surface has the same tone.

The magic of a faux finish lies in altering the thickness of the glaze, either by absorbing or displacing some of the wet glaze with a tool. The feather dusters I'm using here do both. Where the glaze is thinner, more of the white background shows through, creating a highlight. Where the glaze remains thick, less background shows through, creating a shadow. The contrast between highlight and shadow creates the appearance of depth, and the nature of the tool used creates the look of the specific effect. Because a dark-over-light effect usually has a dark tone, these effects are typically bold and dramatic.

Applying a light glaze over a dark base coat usually results in an effect with a soft, subtle look, because the tone of the effect is closer to the light tones typically present in home interiors. A light element in most rooms tends to float in the background, complementing but not distracting from architectural focal points, such as fireplaces or moldings, or from decorating focal points, such as furnishings or artwork.

Now look at the effect you get when rolling a white glaze over a black base coat. Note that the glaze doesn't appear pure white; its translucency allows some of the black base coat to show through. Manipulating the white glaze will allow even more of the base coat to show through, but the tone of the overall result will still be considerably lighter—and thus more subtle—than a dark-over-light effect.

You can use exactly the same tools and techniques with this effect as you can to create the dark-over-light effect—but see how different the two results are! Although the glaze was manipulated in the same way, the light-over-dark effect has a much more subtle look. Its harder to discern the individual impressions of the tools, and the result has a soft, pleasingly out-of-focus appearance. Dark-over-light and light-over-dark techniques are equally effective—they just result in very different looks. If you keep in mind that almost any effect can be done either way, you've doubled your faux finishing repertoire!

seeing is believing

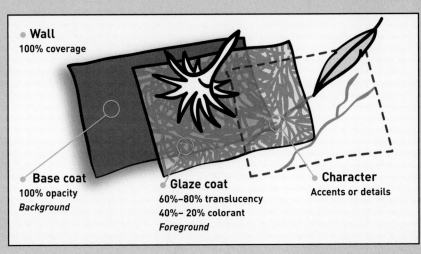

Wall
100% coverage

Base coat
100% opacity
Background

Glaze coat
60%–80% translucency
40%– 20% colorant
Foreground

Character
Accents or details

When you peel back the layers of a faux finish, you can see how they work together to create the illusion of three dimensions. The tools manipulate the paint coats; the combination of background, foreground, and accents fools your eyes into seeing depth.

chapter 4

preparation

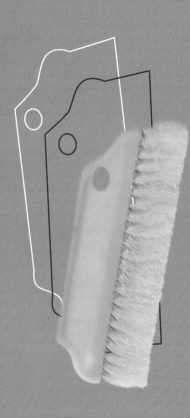

A paint job is only as good as the surface it's applied to, so plan to spend in one to three hours of prep time for every hour spent painting. It sounds like a lot of work, but the more time you spend properly prepping a surface, the faster and easier the application will go, and the better the quality of finish.

Prep makes perfect

Prep work is critical to any paint job. But it is far more important when faux finishing for several reasons:

- **You'll put several layers of finish on your walls,** rather than one or two simple coats. If your paint job fails due to poor preparation, you're out a lot more time and materials than if you had just done a basic, one-color job.

- **Depending on what type of faux finish you choose,** you may be flogging or whacking the wall with stiff-bristled brushes or other tools, or pulling tools across its surface. This stresses the wall much more than a simple brush, roller, or spray application. A poorly prepared surface is less likely to stand up to the rigors of such treatment.

- **Your faux painting may well end up being the focal point of your room**—one that gets a lot of attention. You don't want a poorly prepared surface to detract from the effect.

- **You'll use more materials and tools than with a basic paint job** and you'll work faster. Once you get started it will be hard to stop to fix an imperfection because doing so will interrupt the job and ruin the effect.

- **Faux finishing is a messy job.** All those layers and all that whacking, dragging, flogging, and tapping means that paint will fly—even if you're the type that can paint a room without making a single drip or drop. You'll be glad you took the time to mask and protect surfaces properly.

- **To preserve the continuity of your decorative effect,** it's critical that you have the reach and range you need with each tool. Don't be caught short without the necessary ladder, scaffolding, or extension poles. While it can be inconvenient and risky during a traditional painting job, not having the right accessories can ruin a faux finishing job.

The first step in preparation is to gather the right tools for the job. You don't have to spend a lot of money to create successful faux finishes, but you do need the right equipment.

The key to handling materials is control. Liquids, for example, are always easier to deal with when wet than when dry. So choose tools that control paint and other liquids in their purest, wettest form. Paper dissolves when it comes into contact with water-based materials; metal rusts. Plastic is a great material; it keeps liquids in their wet state and doesn't interact with them, and forms a barrier to protect you and other surfaces. ●

cleaning tools

Use various sizes of **plastic trash bags** and **resealable plastic bags** to store hardware and switchplates. For dusty cleanup tasks, a **shop vacuum cleaner**, a **push broom** with **dustpan**, and **dusting brush** will come in handy. You'll need **5-gallon buckets**, clean rinsing **tile sponges**, a sponge-head **floor mop** with nylon scrubbing pads, and a nylon bristle **deck brush** with extension pole. **Large household sponges** with a nylon scrubbing pad, **2-quart plastic buckets**, and lots of **terry-cloth towels** will round out your cleaning supplies.

Solvents

Solvents dissolve other materials. They are described as cold, warm, or hot according to their degree of volatility, chemical makeup, and use.

COLD. Fabric softener mixed with water dissolves water-based paints. Water-based cleaning products, such as trisodium phosphate (TSP), ammonia, hydrogen peroxide, and all-purpose cleaners, remove dirt and are neutralized with distilled white vinegar. These products are people-safe and earth-friendly.

WARM. Denatured alcohol, acetone, muriatic acid, and rubbing alcohol can dissolve water or oil solutions and are effective surface cleaners if rinsed off well. They are safe when handled, stored, and disposed of properly.

HOT. Mineral spirits and paint thinners, naphtha, turpentine, and lacquer thinner are hot solvents formulated to break down the chemistry of oil-based paints. Be sure to protect yourself and handle these materials with caution. Use, store, and dispose of these hazardous materials properly. ●

cleaning chemicals

Wear heavy-duty gloves and eye protection for safety. Trisodium phosphate, known as **TSP**, is an alkaline cleaner that dissolves grease and deglosses surfaces. To kill mold and mildew, use **hydrogen peroxide**. Use an **ammonia-based** or an **alkaline household cleaner** for removing dirt, and **white vinegar** as a mild acid-rinsing agent. As base material, **baking soda** can create or neutralize chemical reactions. **Muriatic acid** is used to clean masonry. Look for a water-soluble paint cleaner that removes paint from rugs, floors, and woodwork. **Citrus-based cleaners**, such as Goof Off 2, work especially well. **Rubbing alcohol** can clean grease, grime, dirt, and other organic spots from metal hardware. When working with volatile chemicals, use **only nonflammable shop rags** that are specially coated to prevent spontaneous combustion.

rules of tools

Invest in the best. This doesn't mean the most expensive, but rather the most effective tools. Here are a few rules to consider when purchasing tools:

Buy quality, not quantity. Quality wears better and lasts longer.

Buy plastic or stainless-steel products; they are unaffected by water-based or oil-based products. Look for nonporous materials; they're easier to clean up.

Buy brightly colored tools. Fluorescent colored tools are easier to locate and make it easier to avoid mishaps.

Buy plastic containers with airtight lids for short- and long-term storage.

Buy tools that hold you, rather than tools that you have to hold. Easy, stress-free handling and use results in better tool control and less muscle fatigue. Look for ergonomic grips built into a tool.

Protect yourself

Start with the most important tool: you. Never come into contact with paints, stains, or solvents. Why? Because your body is a giant sponge, and you can absorb these chemicals through your skin. To protect yourself, wear nonporous **vinyl gloves**. Latex gloves tear easily and are porous, allowing paint to seep through. Sprinkle **baby powder** into the gloves so they slip on more easily. Wrap a piece of masking tape around the cuff to seal it. To protect bare arms, spray on some **nonstick cooking oil**. It will prevent water-based paint from penetrating your skin. I figure if you can eat it, you can wear it!

For full-body protection, put on **disposable paper coveralls** and a **painter's hat** or **shower cap**. (Bowl covers make great head-protection gear, and they're good for popping over paint buckets to keep the paint from drying out if you pause for a minute during painting.) Wear **goggles**, safety glasses, or a face shield to protect your eyes from dust, chips, or paint; a **dust mask** filters out dust; a **respirator** protects you from dust and chemical fumes. ●

plastic wrap protection

Use plastic wrap as a fast, easy way to cover doorknobs and keep speckles and splatters off hardware and phones. Press a sheet of plastic wrap over your eyeglasses too. You can still see through them, but the wrap protects the lenses from paint drops.

trash-bag apron

Anything you don't want to get paint on, including yourself, should be covered. Here's a painter's apron that's inexpensive, easy to make, and keeps you clean. Lay out a 13-gallon tall kitchen plastic trash bag (a trash compactor bag works best) with the sealed end at the top and open end down. Fold it in half lengthwise. Opposite the folded edge, use scissors to cut off the top corner in an arcing cut to make the armholes (first cut). Make the second cut to create the neck straps, starting about 1 inch below the sealed top edge, cutting parallel about 1 inch in from the first cut. The third cut forms the waist ties. Tie the neck straps together. Save the pouches created by the first cut; you can use them to store a paint can lid.

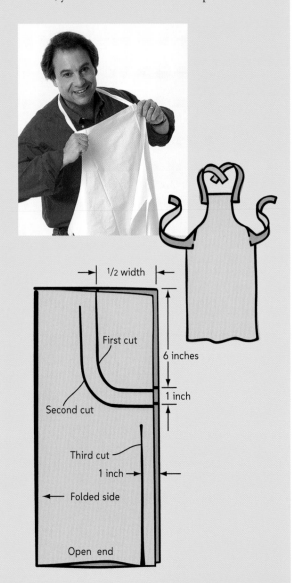

1/2 width

First cut

6 inches

1 inch

Second cut

Third cut

1 inch

Folded side

Open end

Protect the room

Everyone thinks of 2-inch-wide masking tape when it's time for painting. But that beige-colored tape has adhesive that is so sticky, it can sometimes rip the paint and wallcovering right off your woodwork and walls. One of the best things to happen for painters is the development of different types of **masking tapes** designed to perform best with various types of paint. **Blue tape** is designed for latex paints and other water-based finishes. **Purple tape** is for oil-based finishes. **Green tape** is for lacquers. All three stay on regardless of rain and humidity and stick for at least seven days. But the real benefit of these new colored masking tapes is that they pull off any surface—even paint or wallcovering—without causing damage. Colored tape is an insurance policy that protects you from messy mistakes.

Pretaped **masking film** has a built-in cutter and is designed to easily dispense a replaceable roll of masking tape and plastic sheeting. The film unfolds to about 24 inches, providing a drop cloth that protects surrounding surfaces from spills and splatters. The film clings to a surface so it won't flip up into a freshly painted surface, and it is biodegradable, so you can throw it away with the trash. Use **lip balm** to mask glass panes when painting window trim.

Why invest in a big, heavy tarp like the pros use when you'll only use it five times in your life? Instead purchase a **disposable paper/plastic drop cloth**. Face the paper side up to absorb, the plastic side down to protect a surface. This product is nonslip so you won't go sliding across it, and it is biodegradable, so you can wad it up and toss it in the trash when you are finished.

For protecting furniture and other items that are too big to move, use **9×12-foot, .7-mil plastic sheeting** because it provides a lot of coverage. It is inexpensive and biodegradable, so you can throw it away when you're finished. It does have one drawback: it is hard to unfold. Here's a trick: Take the plastic, still in the package, and place it in the freezer for about 30 minutes. This removes the static charge on the plastic, so when you take it out, it's easy to unfold. If you immediately lay it out over furniture, it will wrap itself around the furniture as it warms up. One more tip: Don't use old bedsheets or newspapers when you paint. The paint will go right through them, staining the surface beneath. ●

Tools that rule

The right tools make a project go easier, faster, and safer. Here are a few basics for painting:

- **A 3-in-1 paint can opener is the proper tool to use for opening a paint can.** You can also use it to punch holes in the rim of the can so paint will run inside instead of outside the can and for resealing the lid without damage. Two or three coats of rubber cement keep paint off door hinges and barrels.

- **The basic tool to deliver and manage paint as you apply it to a surface is a 2-quart plastic bucket.** This size bucket is also handy to mix a paint color and to use in cleaning up. For rolling, look for a plastic, square paint bucket with a built-in paint grid. It's a faster, neater way to evenly load your roller. I line mine with a heavy-duty plastic trash compactor bag, secured to the rim with a small bungee cord. I can twist-tie off the top if I need to pause while painting, and when I'm finished painting, I just throw out the empty bag. You also can buy a separate grid to hang in your own bucket (get plastic rather than metal).

- **If you're going to use a conventional roller tray,** get a heavy-gauge metal one; it won't bend when you pick it up the way a plastic tray might. But what about rust and paint contamination? Never pour paint directly into a metal tray. Use a plastic disposable liner or a plastic bag as a liner. You'll save on cleanup time too.

- **Dish soap bottles make great paint delivery containers.** Clear plastic lets you see the paint color. They're easy to grip and squeeze to deliver the paint. The nozzle allows you to dispense the amount of paint you need, then seal the bottle airtight. A plastic paint shield protects a surface while you paint an adjoining wall or ceiling.

- **When painting, use a box fan to prevent fumes from building up.** In a room without ventilation, put the fan in the doorway on the floor to blow fresh air into the bottom of the room, forcing contaminated air up and out the top of the doorway. For rooms with windows, put the fan in a window blowing outward. Open another window or a door (ideally as far from the fan as possible) to create a fresh airflow through the room.

bucket brigade

Have a cleanup bucket ready at the start of any painting project. Why? Because the moment you open a paint can, you risk spilling it. Fill a 5-gallon bucket about two-thirds full of water and place a tile sponge in it. (If you like, you can use a smaller bucket for greater mobility.) Place this bucket in the middle of the room with a large towel beneath it. Use a damp sponge to absorb and clean up any spills; a rag will smear and spread the mess. Change the water often. Have plenty of shop rags or towels around to soak up water spills. Keep several other 5-gallon buckets with lids around for cleaning tools and mixing and storing paint.

PAINTBRUSHES

Paintbrushes are the most basic of painting tools. They spread paint efficiently and are easy to control. If you care for them properly, paintbrushes can last for years. Both of my brushes are more than 15 years old, and except for a paint fleck here or there, they look brand new. To choose your own brush:

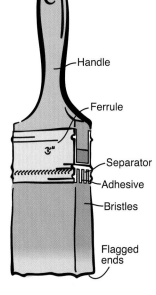

- **Look for one with a sturdy hardwood handle,** a nonferrous or stainless-steel ferrule, and bristles tapered at their end so they form an even line when pressed against a flat surface.
- **Grip the brush by the handle;** the handle should rest comfortably in your palm, fingers on one side of the ferrule, thumb on the other.
- **Fan out the bristles.** Look for flagging: split ends on the bristles. More flagging in the bristles means a brush will lay the paint on the surface better.
- **Flex the bristles.** They should feel springy, not limp or stiff.
- **Use the correct brush for your chosen paint.** If you apply paint with the wrong type of brush, the paint will not flow correctly. For oil-based paints, purchase a china bristle brush. These are natural boar's hair brushes that do not absorb oil but allow it to flow in an even, controlled manner. They are generally black and warm to the touch. For water-based paints, purchase a synthetic/nylon-bristle brush. Water-based paint won't stick to nylon bristles. Nylon bristles are usually beige or cream colored and cool to the touch.

get a grip!

Take the "pain" out of painting. To avoid carpal tunnel syndrome, blisters, and cramps, make a soft grip for your paintbrush. Take 2-inch diameter pipe insulation, trim to the right length, and shove it over the handle of your paintbrush.

This nylon-bristle sash brush is ideal for painting window muntins, sashes, and moldings.

This nylon-bristle brush is designed for cutting-in and trim work with latex paints.

This china-bristle trim brush is angled to help you paint a clean, sharp line when cutting in edges with oil-based paints.

This 4-inch brush holds lots of paint and applies it in a broad swath. It's good for painting large surfaces.

Tools that rule *continued*

When selecting a roller frame, choose heavy-duty plastic or stainless steel. Make sure the handle is comfortable to grip and has a threaded socket in the end so you can add an extension pole. Or buy a frame with a telescoping handle. My favorite has a handle that can expand from 12 to 32 inches, making it easy to roll the wall from floor to ceiling. A 4-foot extension pole works best; it's long enough to help you paint from floor to ceiling, yet short enough to work in a closet. Get a fiberglass handle, not an aluminum one. Fiberglass will not conduct electricity, so if you should happen to make contact with a live outlet or fixture, you won't get hurt. Fiberglass also bends slightly, giving you better feedback on how much pressure you're putting on the roller.

Mini rollers are great. These 4-inch-wide rollers make it easy to paint small, tight surfaces, and they apply paint as evenly as the larger versions. Plus they paint into corners. Corner rollers, which are narrow and tapered to an edge, are ideal for getting into tight corners. The beveled shape and foam material is designed to evenly roll paint on both surfaces of an inside corner.

PAINT ROLLERS

You'll be tempted to buy a cheap, throw-away fuzzy-napped roller, but save yourself the headache! A ½-inch foam paint roller works faster, easier, and better. You can load three or four times the amount of paint onto the roller. Such porosity means less dipping into the roller tray, which means more coverage in less time. Another advantage is that a foam pad will roll over any surface—texture, lap siding, stucco—because it is designed to conform to any surface it touches. A foam roller won't splatter paint or leave fuzzies in the paint on the wall. If you purchase a roller with a nylon core, it is easier to clean, and you can use it over and over. Yellow foam covers are designed for applying water-based paint. Gray or blue foam covers are used with oil-based paint.

PAINT PADS

The 4-inch paint pad is a tool that has everything to offer: It's made of plastic, with a short, thick ergonomic handle. Tracking wheels set off the application pad from adjacent moldings. The bristle face of a pad is perfect for cutting in, edging, and painting flat trim. The pad's foam core holds three times more paint than a brush, has five times more surface area than a regular brush tip, and has bristles that are only ¼-inch long, so the paint won't dry out. It splatters and drips less than a brush. Most pads even come with a plastic paint tray and airtight snap-on lid. ●

Paint grades

When it comes to paint, you get what you pay for, and if you pay for less, you'll get less coverage and lower quality results. It's easy to get confused in the store because there are so many different brands to choose from, each with a variety of additives and enhancers. But in reality, there are only three different grades of interior paint.

LOW GRADE The name says it all: low grade means low price means low coverage. It contains less durable binders and uses clays and other inert ingredients to provide coverage. This type is often referred to as professional-grade or architectural-grade paint. Low-grade paint is requested for commercial jobs in offices or apartments where frequent repainting is standard maintenance. I wouldn't use this as the base coat for a faux finish that I wanted to leave up for years, but as the base for a practice wall that you'll be painting over several times, it's an inexpensive alternative.

MEDIUM GRADE A medium-grade paint, also called decorator grade, contains a range of pigments and binders like those used in the premium grade. Medium grade is slightly less expensive than a premium grade. This kind of paint is an effective substitute for high-grade paint when cost is a factor. Medium-grade paint can be a good choice when you expect to repaint every few years, such as when you redecorate children's rooms. It is also a good choice for low-traffic rooms like guest rooms or those where there is little wear and tear. This paint is fine if you're doing a faux finish in a room that you expect to repaint in a year or two.

Paint grades *continued*

HIGH GRADE When you buy the best, you won't be disappointed. High-grade paint is the most expensive type because of the added pigments and binders. It contains the most solid content of the three—up to 45 percent of the contents.

Yet that doesn't mean that your paint job will increase in price just because you use high-grade paint. Compared with a low-grade interior paint, a high-grade paint will spread more easily, splatter less, and show fewer brush marks. Also, because it contains more pigment, it hides flaws better. In the long run, a high-grade paint can actually reduce the cost of your project because it frequently requires the use of only one coat—a coat that, once dry, has a film that is 50 percent thicker than that of a low-cost paint. The result is a tougher, more durable finish that resists fading, yellowing, staining, and abrasion. These paints are more likely to be scrubbable too.

Many paints marketed at premium prices under designers' names offer special surface textures or effects that can enhance a room. Linen and other fabrics, stone, and other finishes are available in special colors. Some of these paints require special preparation or tools; all call for careful application in accordance with the manufacturer's instructions to achieve the full effect. Durability varies; ask your paint dealer whether the special paint you choose will stand up to your intended use. ●

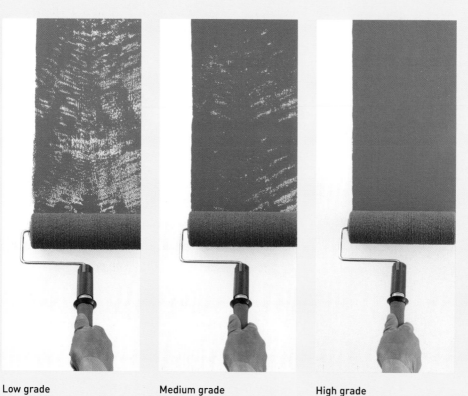

Low grade   Medium grade   High grade

Latex paints offer many advantages over oil-based paints, including ease of application and cleanup, durability, versatility, and low impact on the environment.

Latex or oil?

Paints today are manufactured with very high standards and quality controls that provide the homeowner with great color, performance, and cost-effectiveness. There are two types of paint: latex and oil-based.

LATEX PAINT Latex, or water-based paint, is versatile and easy to use; it dries quickly and cleans up with water (see page 57). It is nonflammable, almost odor-free, and resists fading, cracking, and chalking. A high-quality latex paint has 100 percent acrylic resin as its binder, while a low-quality latex paint has 100 percent vinyl resin. The latter decreases the durability of the paint. A top-quality latex paint has excellent adhesion to a variety of surfaces, including wood, masonry, aluminum siding, and vinyl siding.

OIL-BASED PAINT Oil-based paint dries to a water-tight, impervious film. It goes on smoothly and its colors are deep and saturated. The film is extremely durable and has a greater resistance to fading in sunlight. On the downside, oil-based paints can sag during application. They take longer to dry and turn yellow with age. They can also seal moisture into wood that's not completely dry, causing it to rot. If surfaces are not properly prepared, oil-based paint can crack and discolor.

Oil-based materials and solvents are bad for the environment. Solvent fumes degrade air quality, and both paints and solvents contaminate groundwater if not disposed of properly. Cleanup is more complicated than for latex paints (see page 58). ●

How can I tell what kind of paint is on my walls?

Scrub a small out-of-sight area with detergent, rinse, and towel dry. Using a cotton ball soaked in ammonia, lightly rub the spot. If the paint comes off, it's latex. If not, it's oil-based.

Gloss

Semigloss

Satin

Flat

Behind the *sheens*

Sheen describes the degree of light reflection off the painted surface—in other words, how the paint shines.

Sheen affects the finish's appearance, durability, and suitability for certain uses. As the amount of sheen increases, so does the enamel value, which determines the hardness or protective value of the coating. Manufacturers use many names to describe the different paint sheens, such as eggshell. Because sheens are not standardized, one manufacturer's satin or semigloss paint can have more shine than that of another. Here are the most common finishes:

high-tech flat

Recently, a new paint became available that has the imperviousness to moisture of a semigloss or gloss paint, with the soft, non-reflective surface of a traditional flat paint. Known as "scrubbable flat" paints, these new formulations offer the best of both worlds, giving you a wider range of sheen options for your base coat. I love the stuff!

FLAT paint has the least amount of shine because it has a nonreflective matte finish, which hides surface imperfections. You might think flat paint would make a good choice as the base coat for a faux effect, especially one that imitates stone, wood, or other natural materials. In fact, it's not. Not for aesthetic reasons, but for practical ones. The fact is, flat paint sucks. I'm not being rude; what I mean is that the paint's textured surface quickly absorbs the next layer of paint, so you don't have much time to move it and control the effect. The result can be blotchy. You want more working time, so you need paint with more sheen.

SATIN paint, also known as eggshell, has a soft luster. It still has some texture, but it's more impervious to moisture than flat paint, so the next coat you apply in a faux finishing sequence will dry more slowly than it would on flat paint. This gives you more time to create even coverage, if that's what your effect demands, or to move the paint or glaze around. The traditional base coat for a faux finish is a satin sheen paint, allowed to cure 6–8 hours so the next coat doesn't mix with it.

SEMIGLOSS paint has a higher sheen than satin paint. The light-reflective quality of a semigloss can highlight surface imperfections and cause distracting reflections, so it is generally not a good choice for a base coat. It is, however, an excellent choice for woodwork, doors, and windows, because it stands up to scrubbing and offers a nice textural contrast to a faux finish.

GLOSS paint is the most durable, stain-resistant, and easiest to clean. Its hard, shiny surface is tougher and hides brush strokes. Glossy colors are intense, a characteristic that can highlight surface imperfections and overpower a room. It is also an excellent choice for woodwork, especially in areas exposed to heavy traffic, such as kitchen and bathroom walls, banisters, railings, and cabinets. A clear gloss finish can also be used as a final coat on some faux effects to create textural contrast or to protect the faux treatment from wear, staining, or damage. ●

Tool care

Clean your brushes every two hours while working with water-based paint and at the end of your project.

WASH OUT WATER-BASED MATERIALS

Here's how you can clean water-based paint from brushes and paint pads in 10 seconds:

1. Remove excess paint from the brush or pad by scraping it with the edge of a 5-in-1 tool or the teeth of a brush-cleaning tool.

2. Mix up several gallons of this magic potion in a 5-gallon bucket: For every gallon of warm water, add ½ cup of fabric softener. The fabric softener helps dissolve paint.

3. Dip your brush into the mixture, swish briskly through the water, and count to 10. The paint will release from the bristles and settle to the bottom of the bucket.

4. To dry your paintbrush quickly, use a paintbrush spinner to fling water from the brush. Spin the brush in a wet waste bucket. To make one, start with an empty 5-gallon plastic bucket with lid. Cut an 8-inch hole in the center of the lid. Place a plastic trash bag in the bucket and snap on the lid. The lid keeps the splatter inside the bucket; toss the bag when finished. Rub the tool dry with a small towel.

5. Don't clean the brush with dish soap; it will gum up the ferrule and bristles. And don't rinse the tool in fresh water. Fabric softener coats the handle, ferrule, and bristles, allowing paint to flow effortlessly off the tool. Magical!

6. Follow the same steps for rollers and paint pads. Rollers take a little more time, about 30 seconds, and they might require multiple dippings. ●

1

2

3

4

Tool care *continued*

REMOVING OIL-BASED PAINTS

This cleaning method effectively strips oil-based steps carefully to avoid damaging the brush. You'll need about 20 seconds to clean oil-based paints from a brush, about 30 seconds from a roller.

If you wash out your expensive china bristle brushes in mineral spirits, they will become stiff due to paint residues left inside the bristles. This multi-step washout technique breaks down the oil-based paint and conditions the brush.

1. Start with three clean glass jars (mayonnaise jars, for example) with lids that have a seal. Fill jar No. 1 about two-thirds full of mineral spirits. Fill jar No. 2 with a 50-50 solution of mineral spirits and denatured alcohol. Fill jar No. 3 with pure denatured alcohol. Mark each jar. If you are cleaning paint rollers, paint pads, or other tools that won't fit into the jars, use lidded buckets.

2. Scrape off excess paint using the edge of a 5-in-1 tool.

3. Dip the brush into jar No. 1 and swish it around for about 10 seconds. This is the "hottest" solution and will remove about 70 percent of the paint from the tool. Use a brush and roller spinner to spin the excess out of the brush into an empty bucket.

4. Dip the brush into jar No. 2, swish it around for about 10 seconds, then remove and spin. The mineral spirits dissolve the binders; the alcohol begins to strip out the oils. This will remove about 20 percent more.

5. Dip the brush in jar No. 3, swish for 10 seconds, remove, and spin. At this point, the natural oils have been stripped from the bristles, leaving them brittle and open, so they must be reconditioned.

6. Finish by swishing the brush for about 10 seconds in the liquid fabric softener mixture made following the recipe on page 57. This neutralizes the alcohol and conditions the bristles by restoring their oils. Rub the tool dry with a small towel.

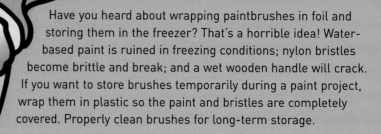

don't try this at home

Have you heard about wrapping paintbrushes in foil and storing them in the freezer? That's a horrible idea! Water-based paint is ruined in freezing conditions; nylon bristles become brittle and break; and a wet wooden handle will crack. If you want to store brushes temporarily during a paint project, wrap them in plastic so the paint and bristles are completely covered. Properly clean brushes for long-term storage.

CLEANING ROLLER COVERS

When you are finished painting, clean the excess paint from the roller cover using the curved edge of a 5-in-1 tool. Follow the directions for cleaning water-based or oil-based paint given on the preceding pages.

DISPOSABLE PAINT ROLLERS

I admit it: Disposable roller covers are more convenient for some jobs. To pull it off the frame, put the roller inside a plastic bag, grab the cover through the bag, pull it off, then seal the bag for disposal. Clean the roller frame appropriately for the type of paint you used. Oil the frame with a little spray lubricant and hang it up.

brush restoration

We all have one—a mucked-up water-based tool that wasn't cleaned properly before it was put away. Here's how to resurrect that old brush so it looks and works as good as new. Mix equal parts water, ammonia, and liquid fabric softener in a glass baking pan. Lay the brush in the mixture for 24 to 36 hours. Take it out and scrub off any stubborn paints. Finish by using the water-based washout method. Repeat until the brush is clean and then store it properly. For a quick solution, use spray oven cleaner; the lye will dissolve the old paint. The most extreme way to clean a tool is to use lacquer thinner, but use this powerful solvent carefully and sparingly.

Tool care *continued*

STORING PAINTBRUSHES

It's not enough just to clean brushes; you should also store them properly to keep the bristles from being damaged. The best and easiest way I know is to slip the dry brush back into its original plastic or cardboard cover. If you threw away the cover, you can make another one from light cardboard. Measure around the ferrule of the brush and add about 3 inches. Cut a piece of cardboard that wide and slightly longer than the distance from the top of the ferrule to the end of the bristles. Wrap the cardboard loosely around the brush and tape it. Slide the brush inside.

If you are as organized as I am, you can even color-code the brush covers. I use red for oil-based china bristle brushes and blue for water-based latex brushes. Finally, hang your paintbrush to store—that's what the hole in the handle is for!

STORING ROLLERS AND PADS

PAINT ROLLERS After spinning and drying the roller covers, the best way to store them is to put them back on the roller frame and hang the roller handle from a nail. That way the roller is suspended in midair and will dry evenly and hold its shape.

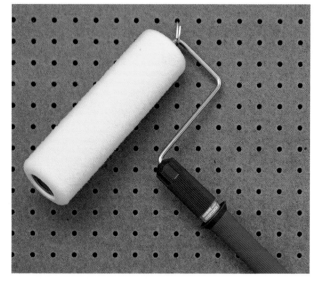

PAINT PADS Some pads are good only for two or three applications, others may last longer—it all depends on the quality of the pad and the type of surface you're painting. Inspect the pads before storing and discard any that show wear (retain the handle and buy a new pad for your next job). To keep the pads fluffy, store them bristle side up. Never store solvent-soaked materials indoors. They release harmful fumes and easily catch fire. ●

Storage solutions

Proper storage preserves the investment you've made in paint and tools, and makes it easier to find everything you need when it's time to begin a new paint project.

STORING PAINT

Store your paint so it lasts a lifetime. Follow these steps:

1. If a paint can is less than one-half full, transfer excess paint to a smaller container. The storage rule is no more than one-third airspace to two-thirds liquid. You can purchase gallon- and quart-size metal paint cans from a home supply store. Pour the paint through a nylon stocking to strain it. Label where you bought the paint, its type, color, sheen, mix number, and the storage date.

2. Using a plastic bag or the leftover curved part of your homemade apron (page 48), cut a circle 1 inch larger than the diameter of the paint can. This plastic circle will serve as a gasket to prevent moisture in the paint from corroding the lid of the can. It also plugs the holes that you punched in the can rim earlier. Most importantly, when you open the can to reuse the paint, you can easily scrape the pigments that have settled on the plastic back into the can.

3. Apply nonstick vegetable spray to one side of the plastic. It lubricates the rim, seals the lid, and prevents a skin from forming on the paint.

4. This step sounds odd, but it is essential in storing paint: Breathe into the can three times. The carbon dioxide from your breath forces out oxygen left in the can. See Law of Painting No. 3 (page 73): The enemy of paint is air (or oxygen, to be more specific).

5. Place the plastic gasket over the top of the paint can, sprayed side down. Gently tap the lid closed using a rubber mallet, which is less likely to deform the lid or rim. Tap the lid flush with the rim. Place a rag over the can before striking to prevent splatters.

6. Store the paint can upside down to keep air from seeping into the can and to prevent a skin from forming. Store paint about 18 inches off the floor in a room, such as a basement, where the temperature averages about 58 degrees year-round. Keep paint locked away from children and never store it near a source of ignition, such as a pilot light or open flame. Both latex and oil-based paints can explode; I've seen it happen. ●

2

5

6

When good paint goes bad

Typically it is difficult to salvage paint that has gone bad, so the best option is to properly dispose of any paint that's old or questionable. That includes paint that is dried out, paint in cans that have rust on the insides, and water-based paint that's been frozen (the paint may look fine, but freezing can cause a chemical change that impedes the paint's binding ability and breaks down its color pigments). Before applying any paint that's been stored for more than a month, smell it. A mildew or earthy smell indicates there's mold growing in the paint, which will inhibit proper application. Dispose of moldy paint too. Then check the paint's consistency. If it is more viscous than new paint, part of its ingredients have evaporated and the paint is no longer usable. If it appears thin or runny, it means that the paint has separated. Old paint has a tendency to separate into its component parts; once it does so, it is difficult to reconstitute it, even with vigorous stirring and shaking. Dispose of it as well. ●

saving dispensed paint

Can you save the paint you poured out of the can? Absolutely, but don't just pour it back into the can from your bucket. Stretch a piece of nylon stocking over the opening of the can to strain any contaminants that dropped into the paint or were carried to it by your brush. Throw away the stocking when finished.

The dish on disposal

Paint products are not as hazardous as they once were, but they still require special disposal. Never pour ANY paint or oil-based solvent down the drain, into a storm sewer, or onto the ground—that poisons the aquifers and our fresh drinking water. Don't throw paint or solvents in the trash in their liquid state, either—in addition to poisoning water, they can catch fire or even explode. Here's how to dispose of paint properly.

OIL-BASED PRODUCTS

Take oil-based paints and solvents to an authorized household hazardous waste disposal site. There they will be processed or recycled so the chemicals in the paint don't pollute groundwater.

WATER-BASED PRODUCTS

Water-based paints and strippers can be disposed of safely in the trash once they've dried. To dispose of them this way, add polymer blue crystal cat litter to the remaining paint in the can and stir until the liquid is absorbed. Leave the lid off the can until the kitty litter hardens, then throw the can of hardened paint and the lid in the trash. Another method is to line a 5-gallon paint bucket with a trash bag, fill it half full with cat litter, then pour the leftover paint into the bucket. When the cat littler has absorbed all the paint and dried, throw the bag into the garbage. With either method, the paint is rendered environmentally safe because the solvents have evaporated and the liquids have turned into a solid state and can't leach into the groundwater.

EMPTY PAINT AND SOLVENT CONTAINERS

Clean oil-based paint cans with paint thinner, allow them to dry, remove their labels, and dispose of them with your recyclable metal cans. Wash out water-based finish containers and do the

same with them. If you don't have a local recycling program, leave the lids off empty paint cans until the paint residue inside dries and then toss the buckets into the trash.

WASHOUT WASTEWATER

Let washout water sit overnight in the bucket. Once the dissolved paint materials settle, gently pour off the water down the sink or toilet. Pour the remaining sludge from the bottom of the bucket into an old, empty paint can and mix it with kitty litter until the liquid is absorbed. Allow it to dry, then dispose of it with the trash. Rinse and wipe out the inside of the wash water bucket with lacquer thinner and allow it to dry.

Proper storage of tools and materials protects your investment in them and sets the stage for an easy start and successful finish to your next painting project.

OIL-BASED SOLVENTS

Oil-based solvents can be stored and used for years if sealed and stored properly. Solvents such as paint thinners can be refreshed and reused repeatedly. That's good for the environment and for your wallet.

When solvents rest undisturbed for several days, the materials in paint will settle to the bottom and the solvents will clarify on top. When the paint materials fill the containers about halfway, pour off the clear solvent for reuse. Leave the lids off the jars and allow the solid material to harden and dry thoroughly, then dispose of them properly as solid waste. Contact your local solid waste disposal office for further information about safely disposing of or recycling leftover paint, used paint buckets, petroleum-based solvents, and other materials.

For long-term storage, place the glass jars in a large plastic storage bin with lid. Mark the bin with red duct tape and write "CAUTION—Oil-based Washout Storage Container—CAUTION" across the tape so there is no mistaking what it is. Tightly pack crumpled newspapers around the glass jars to absorb spills and to prevent glass breakage. After using the container, tightly close

the jars, allow the newspaper to dry out from any spills, and close up the storage container. Store it in a cool, dry, and secure place.

SOLVENT-SOAKED RAGS

Dispose of oil or solvent-soaked rags safely and permanently. Fill a clean, 1-gallon metal paint can two-thirds full with a 50-50 mixture of water and liquid fabric softener. Stuff the rags in the bucket, seal it with a metal lid, and take the filled bucket to a hazardous waste disposal center. The water deprives the rags of the oxygen needed to spontaneously combust, and the fabric softener breaks the bonds of the oils and solvents, making them less volatile. ●

disposal by donation

Instead of disposing of leftover paint at the dump, donate it to your local high school or college drama department, community center, or neighborhood housing organization.

chapter 5

faux *like* a pro

Faux finishes are magical effects. But they're all built on the solid foundation of a well-cured base coat. Before you can do a wash, a wood grain, or a strié, you need to cover the wall with the base coat, using a brush or pad and a roller.

This kind of painting is an easy skill to learn, but the trick to a great job is knowing how to manipulate the tools of the trade. This chapter focuses on choosing materials and mastering a few basic application techniques that will help you produce a professional-looking base coat.

Ready the room

You've probably tried to paint around furniture and carpeting, but it always happens: You dribble or spill paint on something. That's why step one in prep work is to clear out the room. An empty room is an easy room to paint, so begin by removing everything that you can from the room. Gather anything that is left to one side of the room, away from your work area.

- Next, turn off the power to any outlets or fixtures on the surfaces you will be painting. Then remove all light fixtures, switch and outlet plates, heat registers, and towel rods—anything you will have to paint around. This includes drapes (get them cleaned while they are down) and drapery hardware. Don't try to paint around the hardware; it is too frustrating and time-consuming. Just pay particular attention to how your window treatments are attached and make a diagram, if necessary, so you can reinstall them correctly and without guesswork.
- Loosen the canopy or trim piece of a ceiling fixture or chandelier and slide it down the fixture away from the ceiling. Wrap it with plastic trash bags or plastic wrap. Never unscrew a fixture from the electrical box and allow it to hang by its wires. The wires aren't meant to hold a fixture's weight; there's the immediate danger of falling glass fixtures, as well as the risk that the wires could be damaged, creating an electrical short and a fire hazard later. A ceiling fan is impossible to paint around, so take it down.
- Remove switchplates and outlet plates, and protect the switches and outlets themselves with blue masking tape to shield them from paint and moisture.
- Place a worktable in another room, or outside if you will be using solvents for oil-based paints. You can make a table by laying a piece of plywood or a flush wooden door over two sawhorses.
- Place a large, lined trash can in the room to throw away debris as you work. Cleanup is not what you do at the end of the job; it's what you do throughout your project. A messy workplace is unsafe and can slow you down. ●

bag the hardware

I used to have a bad habit of laying switchplates on the floor and losing them under the drop cloth, until I heard "crunch!" Then my wife came up with a brilliant use for resealable storage bags. As you disassemble the room, drop all the switchplates into one medium plastic bag. Remount screws back into their fixtures so they don't get lost or scratch the plastic plates. Separate the hardware for each window, door, and curtain into its own bag and mark its location in the room. Once all the hardware has been bagged and tagged, place the bags into one large bag with the room name on it. For safekeeping, stick the bag on the windowpane of the room with blue tape.

working with a contractor

Sometimes the job you have in mind is too big, too complicated, and too time-consuming to do it yourself. Then the smart thing to do is to call in a professional. If it's the basic painting you need done before you apply the faux finish, talk to a painting contractor. Here are some tips to help you choose a good one.

- Always get written estimates that detail the job, no matter how small.
- Never tell a contractor the price of other estimates you've received.
- Expect a professional job, no matter the cost. If you want it done halfway, you could do it yourself.
- Professionals should be on time. In this day of cell phones, there is absolutely no excuse for someone not showing up when they say they will or at least calling if they will be a few minutes late.
- When an expected contractor arrives, ask to see a contractor's license and a driver's license.

I can't tell you how many people have opened their doors and allowed me to walk right into their homes without asking for proof that I was who I said I was.

- Never let a stranger into your home while you are alone. Call a neighbor or have a friend or adult family member home during the visit.
- Ask to look at a portfolio of the contractor's work and ask for references with phone numbers.

Cleaning

Cleaning a surface before painting is just as important as any of the other steps you've already tackled. One point is worth repeating: An empty room is an easy room to paint. When everything has been removed, clean the floor and baseboards. Cover the floor with plastic sheeting, securing the edges to the floor with duct tape. Then add a layer of drop cloths to protect from splatters. Cover any remaining furnishings with .7-mil plastic sheeting.

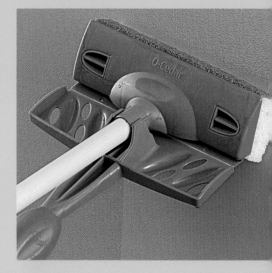

CLEAN THE WALLS

Clean walls are essential for helping paint adhere. The wall should dry for a day before painting. This job is much easier when one person scrubs and another rinses.

First dust off all surfaces with a vacuum cleaner or sweep with a clean dust mop. Set up two separate 5-gallon buckets with two sponge-head mops, one for washing down the surfaces, the other for rinsing off the dirt. Mark the handle of the mop used for washing with red duct tape to prevent mixing up mops when working. Fill your cleaning bucket with 3 gallons of warm water. For every gallon of water add ¼ cup TSP (trisodium phosphate). Mix well. Using a sponge mop with a scrubbing head, wash the wall in 8-foot widths, from the bottom up, working around the room. When you reach your starting point, turn the mop head around and begin scrubbing the wall with the nylon scrubbing head (wet sanding).

No matter what you're washing, change the cleaning solution often to keep from putting dirt and grease back on the surface. After scrubbing the first 8-foot section, use the rinsing solution immediately to remove the dirt and the cleaner off the surfaces. Fill your rinsing bucket with 3 gallons of warm water. For every gallon of water add 1 cup of distilled white vinegar (a mild acid). Mix well. Using the rinse solution, wipe down with the second mop. Change this solution often. The vinegar acts as an astringent and neutralizes the phosphors that could prevent the paint from bonding properly to a surface. ●

grime time

Think your walls are grime-free? Try this test: Spray a tissue with water and lightly rub it on the wall. See that brown smudge? It's body oils, hair spray, and food oils that become airborne while cooking and eventually settle on the walls. Many paint jobs fail because new, clean paint is applied on top of dingy, dirty surfaces. Clean before you paint.

Masking

This last prep step, covering exposed surfaces to protect from splatters and spills, makes painting faster and easier. Think of masking systems as an inexpensive insurance policy that protects you from messy mistakes.

FAUX FINISHING IS A MESSY PROCESS

If you're flogging or whacking, your tool will hit the adjoining surfaces—it has to for a continuous effect. Think of the protection you need for faux finishing versus basic painting as the difference between what you need to keep yourself dry in a gentle drizzle as opposed to a furious wind and rainstorm. An umbrella might be sufficient for the drizzle, but you need a full rain jacket, gloves, and boots to stay dry in a real northeaster.

That's because, unlike basic painting, you risk producing wide-ranging, multicolor paint splatters that can be very difficult to clean or touch up. For example, if you get blue glaze on an absorbent white popcorn ceiling, the only solution is to repaint the whole ceiling. The obvious alternative is good masking.

MASKING ISN'T FUN

Everybody hates it. Pros hate it, especially, because we do it so often and because faux finishers enjoy creating the finish—not prepping the room. But we do it, and do it meticulously, because we've experienced what happens when we don't. The result, we remember, wasn't pretty, or timesaving.

Plus the pros know that once the preparation is done, we can concentrate fully on creating the desired effect, without having to worry about drips, splatters, and misplaced paint. Here's how we do it:

- Dispense masking tape in as long a continuous strip as possible to prevent the paint from seeping between any gaps.
- Firmly press the edge of the masking tape as close as possible to the corner or line that separates one surface from another. Run a plastic tool quickly along the edge to set and seal the tape to the surface. For greater splatter protection, leave the tape sticking out away from the surface.
- Masking film is a powerful prevention system. Dispense and cut the film in one continuous strip from corner to corner. Set the tape firmly. Gently unfold the plastic and smooth it to the surface. The film clings to a surface so it won't flip up onto the fresh paint.
- Wait an hour after painting, then remove the tape and sheeting and dispose of it properly. It is biodegradable, so you can throw it away with your regular trash. ●

1   2   3

Sealing walls

If you are painting the ceiling or sanding a room, this essential step protects walls and woodwork from debris and drips.

1. **Firmly press** the top edge of blue masking tape along the top of the walls.

2. **Slip the edge** of the plastic sheeting under the open tape and press the tape down onto the plastic. The sheeting should drape down over the walls and baseboards. This technique can be also be used to create a barrier between adjacent rooms to contain dust and fumes to the work area.

3. **Heat-seal** the masking tape. This is the secret to keeping paint from seeping underneath the edge of masking tape. Run a tapered plastic tool quickly over the applied edge of the blue masking tape after you've set the tape. This heats the edge of the tape, melting the waxy adhesive on the tape. When it resolidifies at the edge, it creates a barrier that prevents paint from seeping underneath the tape.

Do not remove the sheeting until you are finished with the preparation, painting, and cleanup stages of your project. ●

TV vs. reality

"But the folks on those reality decorating shows never mask," you say. "Why should I?" Good question. But do not take lessons in process from what you see on entertainment television! As a faux finishing contractor, I'd be fired if I did things the way you see them done on those reality decorating shows: no masking, no waiting for dry time between coats, people doing five things to a room at a time... trust me, these shows are for entertainment, not instruction. There's simply no substitute for following the steps. Rush things, and the result is a mess. It may not show up on your TV screen, but it sure will on your living room wall.

Prepping paint

Take the time to box, strain, and condition your paint before you use it, and you'll be rewarded with easier application, more consistent faux effects, and a higher-quality, longer-lasting finish.

BOXING

If you have several cans to use for a job, the color can vary from can to can. Ensure a uniform color by mixing all the paint together, a technique known as "boxing."

Pour all the paint into a clean plastic 5-gallon bucket. Mix it until it is uniform in color. Pour the boxed paint back into the cans. Tightly seal the lids on all but the can you're ready to use.

STRAINING

Straining eliminates lumps in the paint. If the paint has separated, stir the thick paint up from the bottom of each can to free as many lumps as possible. Then box the paint, pouring it all together through a nylon paint strainer and into the bucket.

Paint less than one year old usually doesn't require straining. Older paint might have a thick skin on the top; remove the skin and set it aside. Box the paint, pouring it through a nylon paint strainer into the bucket. When the skin has dried, wrap it in newspaper and discard.

CONDITIONING

Paint stored for a year or longer may need conditioner to improve its flow, adhesion, and coverage. New paint can be conditioned too. The conditioner adds elasticity and retards drying, making it easier to maintain a wet edge during painting—important for reducing overlap marks. I use paint conditioner on almost every job I do.

Following the manufacturer's instructions, add a conditioner such as Floetrol to water-based paint; add Penetrol to oil-based paint. Most paint that is more than three years old should be tossed out (see page 62)—unless, of course, you stored it using the special techniques on page 61! ●

the three laws of paint

To ensure easier application, reduce your chances of accidental spills, and keep paint fresh for a high-quality job, keep these three laws in mind. Here they are— along with why they're so important:

DON'T PAINT OUT OF A CAN.

- **It contaminates the paint.** As you paint, your brush picks up dust, grease, grime, and other contaminants. When you dip into the can to reload, all that debris ends up back in the can, contaminating the paint. That causes flecks and specks in the finish.

- **It dries the paint, making it harder to apply.** If you ever have painted from an open, full can, you probably noticed as you worked that the paint became gooier, stickier, and thicker. This is the air reacting with the exposed paint, which is setting up in the can, not on the wall.

- **It's an accident waiting to happen.** A paint can is strictly a storage and delivery container. It was never designed to be painted from or carried around; it's too awkward and heavy. You are more likely to knock it over and spill, especially the gallon size.

1

72

2

POUR NO MORE THAN ½ INCH OF PAINT INTO A PLASTIC BUCKET FOR APPLICATION.

- **You refresh paint more often,** keeping it in its liquid state for better flow and bond to the surface.

- **You carry less weight,** work faster with better control, and avoid fatigue by the end of the job.

- **You're less likely to spill.** If you have only ½ inch of paint in the bucket, you're less likely to spill the paint if you stumble. And if you do spill, there's less to clean up.

3

AIR IS THE ENEMY OF PAINT.

- **Air is the drying agent for paint.** Paint doesn't dry in a sealed paint can, but the minute you open the can, air rushes in and starts turning the paint from a liquid to a solid, thickening the material, creating drag during the application, and producing an uneven finish.

- **Limit the paint's exposure to air.** Do this by immediately replacing the lid on the paint can after dispensing it and while you're painting. To seal a can for storage, use the techniques described on page 61.

1

4

2

5

3

6

Readying the paint

1. **Gently open the paint can.** Do not use a screwdriver; it will distort the lid, making the can harder to reseal later. Dab a spot of the paint on the side of the can and on the top of the can lid. This quickly identifies the type of paint sheen and color inside the can so you can find it again later.

2. **Slide the wet paint lid into a plastic zip-closure bag** or the plastic pouches left over from making a trash-bag apron (see page 48). Sliding the lid into plastic prevents the paint from drying, stops the lid from dripping paint, and provides a clean lifting tab to be able to open, pour, and close the can as needed.

3. **Punch holes in the groove inside the rim,** called the lid well, with a hammer and nail or with the sharp point of the 5-in-1 tool and a mallet. The holes allow excess paint to drain back into the can. This technique will also ensure that after the project is finished, the lid can set and seal properly into the can for storage.

4. **Lightly stir the paint** (assuming the paint has been mixed on a commercial paint-shaker by your paint dealer).

5. **Pour only ½ inch of paint** into the paint pot.

6. **Place the lid** back on the paint can. ●

line your paint pot with a large resealable bag

Open the mouth of the bag and pull down over the edge of the bucket rim. Secure with a large rubber band. Now, if you need to pause from painting, the bag can be closed to prevent drying. If you need to change colors, drop in a new bag. Cleanup is a snap—just throw the used bag away.

For safety's sake

Take every step possible to protect yourself from potential disasters. Here are some reminders:

- **Shut off the power** at the circuit breaker for the room you are painting.

- **Follow the manufacturer's instructions** and safety precautions for all products.

- **Keep paint products out** of the reach of children.

- **Protect your eyes** by wearing safety glasses or goggles when working overhead, using strong chemicals that may splash, or creating or cleaning up dust. Wearing a full-face shield is also a good idea when working overhead or with solvents.

- **Turn off all sources of flame,** including pilot lights, when using any solvent-based compound or paint.

- **Secure all scaffold planks.** Extend the plank 1 foot beyond a support at each end and clamp or nail it into place. Do not step on the plank between its support and its end.

- **Create a proper, secure storage area** where you can keep materials and tools, especially sharp ones, when not in use.

- **Don't work with solvent-based chemicals** if you are pregnant or have heart or lung problems.

- **Rinse oil- or solvent-soaked rags** and spread them out to dry—don't wad them up. Dispose of them carefully. If you want to reuse rags, launder them thoroughly and spread them out to air-dry.

- **Open the legs of a stepladder fully,** lock the leg braces, and make sure the ladder sits level and steady on the floor.

- **Never stand on the top step** of a stepladder, its braces, or work shelf.

- **Never let small children near open containers.** Always cover a 5-gallon bucket with a snap-down lid.

- **Step down and move** the ladder instead of reaching or stretching.

- **Position an extension ladder** so the distance between its feet and the wall it leans against is one-fourth of the ladder's height. Most extension ladders have a sticker on the side showing the proper leaning angle.

- **Check the manufacturer's label** on your ladder to make sure that it can support your weight plus the weight of the tools or materials you will carry up it.

- **Use a scaffold on stairs.** Place an extension plank on the stairway step and a step of the ladder; make sure it is level. Or use a multiladder in its stair scaffolding mode.

- **Create a flow of fresh air** through the room to prevent fumes from building up. Put a box fan in the doorway or window. ●

no-splatter mixing

Mixing paint yourself can be messy. Here's how to prevent paint splattering as you mix it with a power drill and attachment. Poke the mixer shaft through a paper plate, then hold the plate against the open top of the can while mixing.

Handling a brush

You can spend thousands of dollars learning how to hold a golf club, so it's only fitting that you learn the proper way to hold and use a paintbrush.

HOLD YOUR BRUSH IN YOUR DOMINANT HAND, with your thumb on one side of the ferrule and your fingers spread across the opposite side. You can also grip the brush like a pen or pencil, letting the handle rest comfortably in the hollow where your thumb joins your hand.

USE LONG SWEEPING STROKES to apply and spread out the paint. These broad movements will give you better leverage and minimize muscle fatigue.

AS YOU WORK, KEEP THE TOOL IN FRONT OF YOUR FACE; you will have better physical and visual control.

Loading a brush

Here's how to control the tool and the paint so you load just the right amount of paint onto your brush each time:

DIP your brush into the paint. Since you have only ½ inch of paint in your paint pot, you can't overload the brush bristles or force excess paint into the ferrule.

WIGGLE the brush to load paint into the bristle tips.

PAT both sides of the brush lightly against the inside of the pot as you lift it out. This will release any excess paint from the bristles so they don't drip. Never scrape your brush on the side of the bucket—you can break bristles and damage the tool. ●

TYPICAL GRIP Grip the brush lightly, with your thumb under and your fingers on top of the ferrule. Let the handle rest in the joint where your thumb joins your hand.

ALTERNATE GRIP Hold the brush like a pen or pencil, with the handle resting in the hollow of your thumb joint.

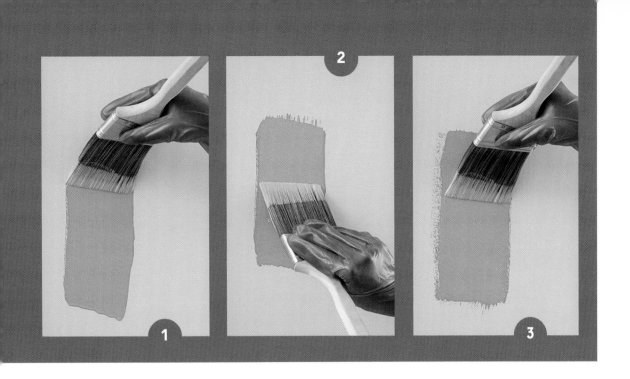

Brush strokes

Gravity is your friend, so work from the bottom of the wall up with strokes about 16 to 24 inches long. Apply the paint in three strokes for a smooth finish:

1. **Stroke up** to unload the brush.

2. **Stroke down** to set the paint onto the surface.

3. **Stroke up again** to smooth the paint and remove brush marks.

Apply the paint quickly, moving up and along the wall, painting from bottom to top, moving forward between strokes. While moving at the end of the last stroke, lift the brush tip off the surface to "feather" the paint back into your wet paint. This step will help the paint blend evenly onto the surface. After you have laid on a section of paint, make one continuous, final stroke to eliminate the overlapping sections and bristle stroke marks. These strokes are enough—don't overbrush the freshly painted surface, or you will gum up the finish. ●

make a power paint pot

Take a 2-quart plastic bucket; make a small hole in the side about 2 inches down from the rim. Fasten a 3-inch pot magnet on the inside with a machine bolt, a nylon locknut, and two fender washers. Put duct tape over the magnet. The magnet will hold the brush by its metal ferrule to keep it from sitting on the bottom of the bucket, which would overload the brush and bend the bristles. Add a flexible handle made from duct tape. Put a short piece, sticky-sides-together, in the middle of a longer piece. Attach the tape to one side of the bucket, around your hand, and up the other side. Remember the tool rule: Make the tool hold you, so you don't have to hold the tool.

Handling a paint pad

A pad is the ideal detail paint tool. A little understanding and practice will help you use this high-tech tool to lay paint faster, better, and more evenly on any surface.

LOOK FOR COMPLETE PAINT PAD KITS. The plastic packaging for the kits is also the loading paint tray and an airtight lid.

MAKE THE TOOL HOLD YOU. Make a flexible handle. Place the empty tray in your hand, palm side up, then stick a piece of tape down one side of the tray, loosely over the back of your hand, and up the other side. Pick up your painting tool in your dominant hand. Grip the pad handle firmly as you paint. Keep the tool in front of your face; you will have a better view of your work and better physical control of the tool.

USE MASKING TAPE. You thought the tracking wheels would eliminate having to use masking tape, right? Wrong. Even though pads are designed to deliver the paint right up to the edge of adjacent surfaces, they are not foolproof. What can easily happen is that when you load the pad, paint gets smeared onto the wheels and they leave little paint marks along the wall or ceiling or trim. Take out some painting insurance—masking tape!

LOAD THE PAD AND TRAY OFTEN. This prevents the pad from drying out.

USE LONG SWEEPING STROKES to apply and spread out the paint. These broader movements will give you better leverage and minimize muscle fatigue.

STORE THE PAD INSIDE THE TRAY if you need to stop painting for a short time. Snap on the lid to stop the paint from drying in the tray.

DIP, WIGGLE, SCRAPE

A paint pad is designed to evenly load and lay paint on a surface. Don't overwork this tool. Here are some techniques that will give you much better control.

DIP the pad into the paint. Pour only ¼ inch of paint into the loading tray. This amount won't allow you to overload the pad bristles or let the pad sink into the paint, or easily spill the tray.

WIGGLE the pad to load the paint into its bristles and foam core. This action will pump in, load up, and lock in the paint.

SCRAPE the pad gently across the edge of the tray. Don't press too hard; you want the bristles to be full of paint, but not dripping. The excess paint will flow back into the paint tray. This lets you control the load amount going onto the surface. ●

different strokes

Gravity is your friend, so work from bottom to top and from side to side with strokes about 24 to 36 inches long. You'll need only two strokes for a smooth finish.

Stroke in one direction to unload the paint in the pad.

Stroke back over the same area in the opposite direction to set the paint and remove bristle marks. At the end of this stroke, lift the pad while moving to feather back into the wet paint. This will help the paint blend evenly onto the surface.

Apply the paint quickly, moving up and along the wall, painting from bottom to top and moving forward between strokes.

Handling a roller

A sponge roller and roller frame are the perfect tools for painting large surfaces. Screw in an extension pole on the end of the frame for better leverage as you work. Here's the best way to hold, control, and use this simple painting system:

MOISTEN THE ROLLER COVER with water (if you'll be using latex paint) or paint thinner (if using oil-based paint). After dampening the cover, wrap a clean shop rag around it and blot dry.

POUR ½ INCH OF PAINT into the paint tray (a plastic-lined metal tray) or a bag-lined bucket and loading grid, if you have a lot of painting to do. Fill a paint bucket no more than one-third full.

ROLL THE ROLLER down the slope of the tray, called the rake, with quick, firm strokes. Gently dip into the paint well to load the tool. Try not to slosh the roller around.

LIFT THE ROLLER directly above the tray and move it back up to the top of the rake. Roll the roller slowly down the slope of the tray. Repeat this procedure

several times to load the cover properly. Try not to spin the roller as you do this; it will splatter the paint. Work the paint deep into the roller. Keep rolling down the rake until the roller is evenly coated with paint but not dripping.

LET'S ROLL

A paint roller is designed to roll paint on a surface; it is not meant to splatter it. Do not overload this tool and do not roll quickly. With the paint roller loaded, approach the wall.

HOLD the roller frame and pole firmly with both hands. Place your dominant hand at the bottom end of the pole for more control. Place your other hand in the middle to act as a leverage point that will mechanically triple the amount of force applied to the roller. As you work keep the tool in line with your body; you will have better balance, stamina, and vision.

POSITION the roller so the open end points the direction you are painting. This keeps the roller from sliding off the roller frame.

APPLY the three-stroke rule:

1. **Roll up** to unload the paint roller. Don't roll too fast. Doing so will cause the roller to splatter paint. Use long, continuous strokes to apply and spread the paint. These broader movements will give you better leverage and reduce muscle fatigue.

2. **Roll down** to set the paint onto the surface.

3. **Roll up again** to smooth out or lay-off the paint finish. As you begin your third stroke up, twist the roller extension pole slightly in the direction you are working. This move puts more pressure on the leading end of the roller—the one that hits the unpainted part of the wall first—to deliver maximum paint where it's needed. It also creates less pressure on the trailing end of the roller, the end on the wet side of the paint job. This helps eliminate the ridges of wet paint (snail trails) that are caused by too much roller pressure.

WORK FROM THE BOTTOM of the wall up. Moving across the wall and working in sections—about three or four roller widths wide and the full height of the wall—continue loading the roller with paint, using the same stroke techniques across the entire length of the surface. Reload the roller cover often. Keep the roller cover moist and saturated with paint. A thoroughly loaded roller cover will make the paint flow more easily, to cover the surface better.

LAY OFF THE PAINT after you have painted about 8 feet of wall by lightly rolling an unloaded roller from the top of the wall to the bottom. This keeps the surface sheen consistent and eliminates the "V" effect when the paint dries.

KEEP MOVING FORWARD. As with any application tool, keep a wet edge of paint. ●

Working a room

It takes two ... two people to effectively paint a room: the cutter person and the roller person.

Choose the right person for the right job. Break down your plan into logical and manageable steps. Identify, define, and divide the workload into separate but equally important tasks. One person uses a brush or a pad to apply a narrow band of paint around the room where one surface meets another. This is called cutting in. The other uses a roller and extension pole to continuously and consistently apply the paint to the large surfaces. This is called rolling out.

If you're detail oriented, handle the cutting in and trimwork. If you're stronger, paint with the roller. Working in a team of two makes the job twice as fast and half as tedious, saving you energy, time, and money.

Stay focused on your assigned task, because the more you do something, the better and faster you become. Your satisfaction level will rise, and your results will look even better.

DIRECTION CONNECTION

If you're right-handed, you will find it easier to paint from left to right. If you're left-handed, work from right to left. Begin painting from the corner behind a door or closet. The cutter paints out from a corner, then the roller comes behind and rolls the paint over the wet cut-in band. Continue working around the room this way.

Of course, one person can paint a room working alone, but it takes much longer, and it's harder to keep the paint flowing and maintain a wet edge. If you must work alone, paint in small, manageable sections and work quickly but methodically. ●

keep your edge

Don't cut-in an entire room and then roll-out the walls. What happened to maintaining a wet edge? It dried, of course, creating visible overlaps. When you apply the wet roller over the dried cut-in band, the paint creates an overlap called "hat banding." To correct this problem you will have to apply two to four coats of paint, which will require more paint, time, and effort.

Hit the walls
CLEVER CUT IN

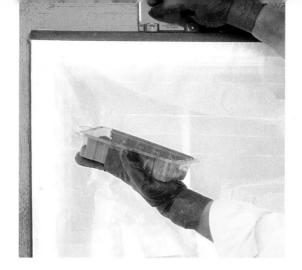

Be sure to mask all surfaces that you don't want to get paint on. Cut-in first, applying the paint swaths about 4 feet ahead of the roller person. Firmly grip the loaded tool with your dominant hand and apply the paint, keeping the tool in front of you. Have a platform ladder handy so you can easily reach all the surfaces.

Working in one direction, lay a 3- to 4-inch-wide band of wet paint along the inside edge of the wall. The wet band creates a dividing line of paint from one surface to the other, a "safety zone" so the roller person doesn't roll too close and get paint on the adjacent surfaces. Work from the bottom up, applying around the edges, first along the baseboards about 4 feet, then up and along the inside corners, and finally across at the ceiling line.

After you have laid on about 5 to 6 feet of paint, make one continuous, final stroke to eliminate overlap and stroke marks. Do not continue stroking the painted surface; doing so will gum up the finish.

Clean small application tools, such as pads and brushes, about every two hours (see page 57).

ROOM ROLL OUT

The roll-out should be applied only after the cut-in has been done and the paint is still wet. Be sure to tape down drop cloths to protect the floor and give you safe and sound footing. Attach an extension pole to the roller frame or use a telescoping handle. Load the roller cover with paint. Position the loading tray or bucket just ahead of your work section to keep you moving forward and reduce your body movements. It also helps prevent roller dripping and bucket spills. Properly load the paint roller and start at the section to be painted. Keep the tool saturated with paint. If you must stop for a time, close up or wrap the tray and roller to keep them from drying.

Body position and mechanics are an important part of fast and effective painting. Stand with your feet spread about shoulder-width apart, always with your body facing the direction you're going to paint. This position, called the "A" stance, gives you better balance and leverage to reach bottom to top in one continuous stroke.

With the roller loaded, position yourself in front of the section you want to paint. Place the roller on the surface and apply the paint to the wall. To avoid paint splatter, don't roll fast, but work at a comfortable rhythm and pace. After you have applied and laid-off two or three roller widths on the wall, take a step forward and repeat the same procedures. The cutter and the roller should be spaced no more than 4 to 6 feet apart; this spacing ensures the roller is always painting into the wet edge. Continue working around the room in this manner until it is completed. ●

don't wait

Pull the masking tape while the paint is fresh! Remove the masking materials within 45 to 60 minutes after the paint is applied and set to prevent surface tear up. The idea of masking tape is to protect surfaces from the paint; however, when you slop the wet paint over the sealed masking tape, then let the paint cure to hard, the paint film bonds to both the wall and the masking tape. As you remove the masking tape, the film acts as one piece, and will tear and rip up the wall or trim work. It's definitely easier to remask an area than to repair it!

Faux get it!

Faux effects are two-dimensional representations of the three-dimensional world. These painted illusions have height and width; the visual depth is created by using optical tricks such as scale and perspective, highlight and shadow. A scenic wall mural, a wood grained door, or a painted inlaid tabletop are all examples of trompe l'oeil effects, a French term that means to fool the eye. If it's not the real deal, it's faux, or in other words, a false finish.

A faux effect is an applied paint technique that simulates materials or imitates natural finishes. With the proper surface preparation, a faux effect can be applied on almost anything. The effects are created by painting a base coat of color, then layering different colors of semitransparent glazes on top of the base coat. ●

depth of field

Faux effects are all about creating visual dimension where there is no physical dimension. Part of that effect is achieved by the nature of glaze itself. Unlike paint, glaze is semitransparent, allowing you to see through the top layer of the finish and glimpse the base coat underneath. But how much depth you perceive—something faux painters call the "depth of field" of a finish—depends on the degree of contrast between light and dark. In general, the higher the contrast between the base coat and glaze, the greater the perceived depth of field.

The tree of knowledge

A simple way to understand how painting relates to faux effects is to imagine a tree. Basic painting represents the roots and the trunk of a tree. Faux effects represent two branches of that tree: positive techniques and negative techniques, both of which we'll discuss at length later. The specialty finishes are the tree's leaves: They're the decorative finishes that everyone sees, but in reality the trunk still holds the tree together. Underneath it all, the root system, or preparation, is what goes unseen but keeps the tree stable. You need to know the basics before you move on to the specialty effects.

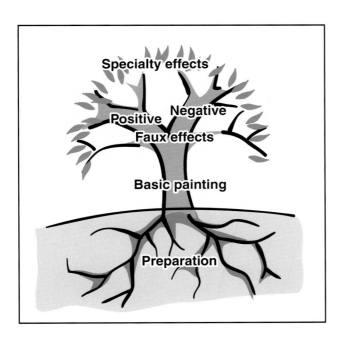

THE THREE C'S

CONCEPT of faux effects refers to the color, style, furniture, and general design elements of a room that will guide you in choosing a faux effect. You must have a clear plan, or concept, to be successful in faux finishing.

CONTROL is a question of mastering the medium. The control is the knowledge you have to produce an effect, as well as the tools that are used in this process. Hair clips, dish soap bottles, and sponge rollers are all examples of devices that help you control, or master, the medium of paint. Another aspect is how you control the ultimate painting tool—yourself. Be patient with yourself and your partner, and understand that you will make mistakes throughout the project. Your failure will ultimately bring success. This doesn't mean you can't experiment. In fact, some of my best finishes have been the result of mistakes. Make sure you feel comfortable and confident with the technique and tool before tackling an entire room. Remember, when you believe, you can achieve the magic.

The result of how much control you have is what **CHARACTER** is all about. The character of the effect is the end result of your project. It's a combination of planning, procedures, and the choices you make in your project partner, your faux finish tool, and your willingness to practice and make mistakes. You must be happy with your results; if not, keep practicing until you are satisfied with the character of your project. ●

Have no FEAR

No FEAR—No **F**rustration, No **E**ffort, No **A**nxiety, and No **R**esistance to a project. Surprisingly, your greatest successes arise when you turn yourself over to the realm of possibilities. With No FEAR, a Wizard can move to the next step of taking RISKS. That means taking **R**esponsibility, taking **I**nterest, taking **S**elf-control, taking **K**nowledge to understand the project, and taking **S**atisfaction away from the project. When you take RISKS, you'll reap the rewards. The more you do, the better you get. Wizards aren't afraid to fail. They call it practice, and the more they do it, the better they get.

The right tools

In addition to common painting tools such as paintbrushes, rollers, and plastic paint pans, decorative finishes require specialty tools to create certain effects. But that doesn't mean you have to go out and spend a hundred bucks for a leather-look kit. In fact, some of the wackiest household tools create the most luxurious faux finishes. Remember to think off the wall and out of the can.

The Right Tool Rule states that things with handles, things made of plastic, and things that leave an impression are the most suitable for creating simple faux effects. A tool with a handle gives you a mechanical advantage, and it distances you from the surface you are working on. Why does this matter? You can see the effect emerge more clearly, and you keep yourself from being covered with glaze. Plastic is the easiest

material to clean. Things that leave an impression offer an array of finishes that play upon highlight and shadow and create the optical illusion of depth in your faux effect.

It is also important to consider scale and perspective when choosing a tool to make an impression. The larger the tool, the larger the imprint. If used in a small room, a large tool can create a dramatic and sometimes overwhelming effect. When used in a larger room, the impression is proportional to the space. ●

bigger tool, bolder effect

Size does matter! In conventional painting, tool size relates purely to applying paint in the most accurate, efficient manner. Faux painting, however, uses varying size tools for varying effects. Here a broom-and-squeegee tool sold to spread and level driveway sealer is used to create a striated pattern. Cut notches in the rubber squeegee side and draw it down the wall to create a big, bold stripe pattern—in no time!

Cool tools

When searching for a tool to create an effect, look for items made of plastic that have textural elements like bristles and fabric or a raised surface. Also look for items with a handle for ease of use. If you will be working on a large surface, look for large items. For example, a large, industrial dust mop will cover the surface in less time than a standard dust mop. A note: Buy two of the same tool so that you will always have one to use and one that is drying while you work.

Here are some other tools to consider:
- Toilet brush
- Tongs
- Flyswatter
- Truck tire brush
- Duster car mop
- Sea wool sponge
- Squeegee
- Bubble wrap
- Terry cloth
- Barbecue brush

As I mentioned earlier, sometimes the wackiest items make the best effects. Where do I look for tools? In the automotive and household cleaning sections—you'll never look at Kmart or Wal-Mart in the same way again!

Sealer

Base

Glaze and effect

What lies beneath

Regardless of the effect you want to create, the first step in faux finishing is to paint a base coat on the wall. If you are a novice, begin with only two colors, then incorporate more complex combinations as you master a technique. Follow three rules when choosing a base coat:

- Always paint the darker color on the wall. OK, maybe not always, but if you're a novice, it is so much easier if the dark color is on the wall because it is easier to lighten a color than darken it. Use the lighter color in the top coat of glaze. This creates the illusion of a three-dimensional surface with highlights on top and shadows underneath.
- Use satin or eggshell interior latex paint for your base coat. Flat paint sucks—literally—because of its high porosity; it has no sheen value. On the other hand, satin latex paint has a slight sheen that is ideal for decorative effects.
- Allow the base coat to dry completely before applying the top coat of glaze, a minimum of 4 to 8 hours. If you don't, the chemicals in the top coat of glaze can dissolve the base coat of paint. I usually paint the base coat the day before I create the faux finish. ●

quiz the wiz

How far in advance can I paint the base coat?
You can wait no more than a week before painting your faux finish on top of your base coat. Waiting longer will jeopardize the paint job because of everyday contaminants, such as hair spray, cooking oil, and general dust buildup. These contaminants put a film on the clean surface and prevent proper adhesion of the glaze.

What if I already have a satin finish on the wall?
You can apply glaze over an existing satin finish, but you need to clean it with a TSP solution first (page 68).

That glazed look

Glazes modify the color of a base coat of paint by allowing it to peek through a translucent filter. Think of glaze as the lens in sunglasses. You can see through a tinted lens, but the view is altered. Use a glaze when you want to create visual depth of highlight and shadow.

Here's the main reason people buy this book—for the recipe of my amazing Wall Wizard Glaze. If you mix as directed, you'll have the perfect potion for faux finishing.

- **One-half quart satin or eggshell latex interior paint.** Remember to use the lighter color of your two-color combination.
- **Two quarts glazing medium.** This glazing medium is actually paint without color. It pulls the paint color molecules apart to create the translucent or semitranslucent effect of glaze.
- **One-half quart water.** Water is the thinning medium that makes it easier to work with the glaze.
- **6 ounces Floetrol.** A binding medium, Floetrol is a Wall Wizard wonder. It stops blistering, cracking, mold, and mildew. It makes the color last three to four years longer, and it conditions the paint, making it sticky and gooey so the glaze sticks to the wall without running. Floetrol can be found at any home supply store.
- **4 drops fabric softener or ¼ teaspoon per gallon of paint.** This household product acts as an extending agent, preventing the glaze from drying too quickly.

Combine all ingredients in a clean, 1-gallon juice jug and shake for about three minutes before using to keep the mixture from separating. In fact, every time you pick up the jug or dish soap bottle, give it a shake before using— just make sure the lid is sealed tightly.

A 1-gallon juice jug makes the perfect container because it is made of plastic, so it won't corrode. It has a handle and an airtight seal, both of which are ideal for storing paint. And it holds enough glaze for 1,500 square feet, which will cover approximately two 10×15-foot rooms.

To make more or less glaze, use 1 part paint color to 4 parts glazing medium. The remaining ingredients are proportionate to this recipe.

How much glaze do you need? Enough to cover your project! Seriously, you will never ever be able to match a paint color, so if you run out of glaze before you finish, you might as well start over. Always make twice as much glaze as you think you will need. ●

dishing up glaze

Instead of lugging around a gallon of glaze, fill a 1-quart dish soap bottle. The bottle has an airtight seal, it's easy to control, you can squeeze out just the amount you need, and most importantly, if you drop it, you won't get glaze all over everything!

Clean as you go

Cleanup is not the last thing you do; it's what you do throughout your paint project. Here are some helpful tips to keep your work area clean and your job progressing smoothly:

- **Maintain your work space.** Centralize the tools in one area. Place them on your project table so you can find them throughout the job.
- **Clean frequently.** Wipe down, sweep, and vacuum often so debris will not settle into the surface finish.
- **Clean up any paint splatters or spills immediately.** It is easier to absorb up wet paint than it is to chisel off hardened paint.
- **Throw out trash as you generate it.** Set up a large, lined trash can in a convenient location. Constantly pick up and throw away used masking tape, plastic wraps, and other debris as you work. Having a messy work space prolongs the job and makes it more dangerous. ●

Team works!

Teamwork applies to the final phase of your painting project.

DIVIDE TO CONQUER. Identify, define, and divide the various tasks into logical and manageable steps. Working in a team of two makes the job twice as fast and half as tedious, saving you energy, time, and money.

STAY FOCUSED. Stick to your assigned role and task Clean from the ceiling down, working down and out of the room.

BE THOROUGH. Observe and repeat procedures to ensure quality control. ●

Reassemble the room

Once the work is finished and the paint has dried, remove all the coverings and clean the room again. Remount all the switchplates, towel bars, drapery hardware, vents, and grills. Turn the power back on at the circuit breaker panel. And finally, take a moment to admire your handiwork and enjoy the beautiful colors and finishes. But not too long; you have more cleanup to do. ●

spin 'em dry!

Just because a brush and roller spinner is so much fun to play with doesn't mean it's not a practical tool. In fact, this tool cuts drying time for brushes and paint rollers to about one minute. Simply push your brush or paint roller into the spinner, pump the handle, and voilà! The water is eliminated from the bristles or roller.

Positive thinking

Faux finishes can be divided into either positive or negative techniques. Loading a tool with glaze and applying it to the wall is a positive technique—you are adding glaze to the wall. Covering the wall with a coat of glaze and then using a tool to remove it is a negative technique because you are taking glaze away. No matter which faux finish you want to achieve, you will use either a positive or negative technique to do so.

Positive techniques in decorative finishing are the hardest to achieve because you have to get the effect even. It requires tactile response, the feedback you receive from the pressure you put on the tool. More pressure on the tool creates less detail because the tool, a sponge for example, is compressed against the wall. Less pressure creates more detail, because the points of the sponge surface make contact.

It usually takes three tries to get the hang of a technique: Your first try will be a failure, your second will be better, and by the third you'll start to see the effect you want.

1. Lay out two plastic plates and squeeze glaze onto one. Use masking tape to attach the other to your "off" hand.

2. Load the tool by dipping it into the glaze three times: "Dippy, dippy, dippy."

3. Unload or lighten the load of glaze on the tool by tapping it on a clean plate three times: "Tappy, tappy, tappy." This also serves to distribute the glaze evenly on the tool.

4. Gently touch the wall with the tool, keeping your hand parallel to the wall as you work. The tool should move perpendicular to the surface.

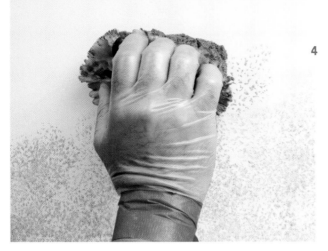

4

5. Rotate your wrist one-quarter turn as if you were turning a doorknob. Your process repeats over and over: Tap, pick up the tool, rotate, tap, pick up the tool, rotate, and so on, turning your hand to a different position each time. Reload the tool.

Work in a spiral motion in 4-foot sections instead of straight across to avoid making a pattern. Work from the bottom up and into your field of view. A positive finish looks best when it is randomly applied on the surface. Avoid creating rows, columns, or any sort of structure in the finish. ●

5

get a handle on sponging

Clamp a hair clip to a sponge to create the perfect handle. Clips are made of plastic, they make the sponge ergonomic so it's easier to hold, and they make it simple to control the sponge during application. Clips make it a cinch to sponge in corners and hard-to-reach areas.

tips 'n' tricks

• Start on a practice wall to master your technique. Laundry rooms and guest rooms are a good choice—not the living room or kitchen where your mistakes will be visible. Be sure to prep the wall.

• Always dampen your tool in a solution of fabric softener and water (page 57) to prevent the glaze from sticking to the tool. The solution also softens the tool to make the paint application easier. To make sure the tool is not too wet, cover the tool with a towel and wring out the excess solution.

• Make sure the molding is covered with tape or plastic so you can get into corners with your faux finish tool.

• Have two tools on hand: one to use and one that is drying while you work. When one tool is saturated with paint, clean it in a solution of fabric softener and water, then use the other tool while the first one dries.

Negative finishes

Negative techniques require two roles to create a successful faux finish: the glazer and the whacker. The glazer applies glaze to the wall from the floor up. The whacker "whacks" the wall from floor to ceiling with the tool to create the effect by removing glaze. You can do negative finishes solo, but the technique really works much better when you team up with another person.

Working as a pair makes the job go more quickly; you get better results when working in assembly-line fashion. The glazer cuts-in and rolls on the glaze; the whacker works 4 to 6 feet behind the glazer. Don't let one get too far ahead or behind; the glaze will dry and you will get out of rhythm.

Changing whackers in the middle of a project will completely change "the hand" (the effect), because different people apply different pressure and rotate their wrists differently while whacking a wall. If you must work alone, work in 4-foot-wide sections, floor to ceiling, so the glaze doesn't dry while you are applying the faux effect.

One of the great things about negative finishes is that if you make a mistake—while the glaze is still wet—you can simply "erase" it by reglazing over the area and whacking it again.

Above all, make sure you practice, practice, practice your techniques. The moment of truth comes when you apply the glaze to the wall for the first time. If you're already accustomed to working with the glaze, your results will be dramatically better. ●

rhythm and time

Rhythm is an important part of faux finishing. Getting in the groove—that is, pacing and timing your application as you paint—will help you control and create consistency throughout your effect. It's all about keeping the glaze wet from one section to the next as you work vertically and horizontally across the wall with your tool. A tip: Play music while you work. It makes it easier to establish rhythm in your technique.

Also make sure that you work in the direction in which you feel most comfortable. If two people are working on a project, then you both need to work in the same direction; it will be easier to keep your rhythm, balance, and coordination. And try to work directly in front of yourself—your field of vision and your control of the tool will be much better.

Rag-rolling

1. Using an application tool (such as a brush or pad), cut in the first section of the wall to be glazed. This section is generally 4 to 6 feet wide, working from floor to ceiling.

2. Pour ½ inch of glaze into the well of a paint pan. Load a sponge roller evenly with glaze.

3. Working from the bottom up, apply glaze to the wall over the base coat. Use more pressure on the lead side of the roller to avoid snail trails in the paint. The goal is to create an even, consistent coat of glaze on the wall.

4. To create the faux effect, begin removing glaze with the tool, working from the baseboard up in 4-foot-wide sections, 4 to 6 feet behind the glazer. Roll randomly at all different angles, picking up the tool between each stroke. Work continuously around the room in sections. If you must stop working, stop in a corner where the change won't be as apparent. If you are right-handed, you'll probably find it easier to work from left to right. The opposite is true for left-handers. ●

wet and dried

Can the base glaze dry before adding the second layer of glaze?

Yes, dry stacking creates crisper patterning with stronger details.

Can I apply a second layer of glaze onto a wet coat of base glaze?

Yes, but only in small amounts and contrasting colors. Wet blending creates softer effects.

working with a professional faux finisher

Perhaps, after reading this book, you want to hire out some or all of the faux finishing you have in mind. I always encourage people to try it themselves, start in an inconspicuous place, practice, practice, practice, and then move on to more public spaces in your house. But we all have demands on our time and attention, and there's nothing wrong with calling in a pro. If you do, take the responsibility to thoroughly check out any finisher you're thinking of hiring before contracting the job.

WHEN CHOOSING A FAUX FINISHER, follow all the tips on page 67. In addition:

- **Look for a finisher who** treats his or her work like a business. Their dress, demeanor, even the condition of their vehicle should be neat and professional, and they should be interested in listening to you and working with you to get the results YOU want.

- **Respect, but don't be intimidated** by their artistic knowledge. Ask questions, and if you can't get something explained to your satisfaction, choose another contractor.

- **Ask to see a portfolio** of their work—not just photos of jobs they've done, but also actual finishes painted on demonstration boards.

- **Ask for references** of previous customers. If possible, visit these customers to look at the job. Ask the customer if they were satisfied with the work, if the results were as agreed upon, if communication was good throughout the job, and if the contractor was neat, careful, and on time.

GET EVERYTHING IN WRITING. Once you select a faux finisher, you need to agree to a contract that covers all aspects of the job:

- **Determine who is responsible** for doing the prep work. If the contractor will do the prep work, spell out specific tasks in the contract. If you're responsible for the prep work, understand clearly what's expected of you. I always use two colors of chalk to mark up any walls in a client's house they are responsible for prepping. One color shows areas that need to be sanded, another shows areas that need to be filled. If you're going to do the prep work, have the contractor sign off on your job once you've finished it, agreeing that you performed the work properly.

- **Understand what condition the wall,** room, and work space are to be in upon the contractor's arrival. I hand clients a sheet detailing the condition I expect the work space to be in when I arrive, along with a price sheet listing how much I'll charge if I have to, for example, clean a bathroom or remove furniture from a living room.

- **Discuss the nature of the effect** you desire and the means used to create it thoroughly. Then have the finisher create "story boards" for each effect: I create the effect I'll use on each surface on pieces of 24×30-inch foam-core board, so the client knows exactly what they're getting. After we sign the contract, I cut the story boards in half and the client and I both initial each half of every board. I keep one set; the client keeps the other. That way we're both protected against subjective interpretations of the desired outcome. If the wall matches the board, I've delivered on the contract.

AGREE ON A PAYMENT METHOD. There are four common ways to calculate the cost of a job. All have advantages and disadvantages:

- **Time and materials.** Under this method, you pay for the materials necessary to do the job—paints and other expendables—and a fixed, per-hour rate for the contractor's time. This method keeps the cost of a job in proportion to the contractor's effort, and gives the client an incremental way of keeping track of expenses. On the other hand, it gives the contractor little incentive to work quickly. Contractors who lack the experience required to submit a bid most often use this method. It can result in a lower cost job, but does not necessarily do so.
- **Square footage price.** Using this method, you pay a fixed rate per gross square foot of room size for a given effect. Simple effects cost less per square foot; complex, multistep finishes cost more. This allows both parties to know the cost of the job up front. As a homeowner, though, you need to be aware that the square footage used is gross square footage—there's no deduction for windows, doors, cabinets, built-ins, or other elements of a room that will not get the finish. That's because it's often more time-consuming to mask off and paint around these elements than it would be to paint bare, uninterrupted walls in a room of an equivalent size. The advantage is that as a consumer you know in advance the price you'll pay; the disadvantage is that an expert contractor might—but might not—be able to give you a better deal with a fixed rate, depending on the precise nature of the job.

- **Bid price.** Using this method, the faux finisher gives the consumer a fixed price to complete the job. The advantage is as a consumer, you know exactly what the job will cost. The advantage to the contractor is that a single bid price rewards proficiency and efficiency. Veteran contractors who can produce expert work quickly and estimate job times and costs accurately in advance usually use this method, as it's more profitable. It may or may not result in a job cost that's higher than the time and materials method.

- **Bid plus time.** When it comes to creating elite effects, such as adding trompe l'oeil accents on top of a faux finish, an experienced contractor will often charge a fixed rate to do the underlying finish, then charge an hourly rate to produce any additional elite effects requested by the customer. That's because "painting a few birds in a tree in the corner" can be interpreted many ways, and it can be hard to estimate the time required to execute the job to the customer's satisfaction. The hourly rate ensures that the amount paid for the effect is proportional to the time required to execute it. ●

faux effects

Now that you've been introduced to faux painting tools, materials, cleanup, as well as some basic application techniques, you're ready to enter the world of faux finishing. We'll start off with some basic effects, such as sponging and ragging. Then we'll move on to more involved effects, such as woodgraining and marbling.

How absorbing!

Sponging is what most people think of when they think of a faux finish, and for good reason: it's a versatile and attractive effect.

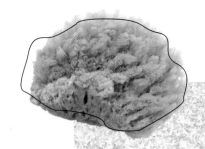

sponging

SPONGING IS THE ICONIC FAUX FINISH TECHNIQUE—the softly stippled, almost impressionistic look it creates is among the most recognizable and widely useful of all faux finishes. It creates a soft background that is a great foil for solid, geometric elements within a room. Spaces with lots of molding; strong architectural elements such as dormers, windows, doors, and built-ins; or rooms that feature bold furnishings or artwork often benefit from sponge-finished walls. Such walls can be ideal hosts: they increase a room's sense of space. Given the right choice of base color and glaze, they can also harmonize a room's many different elements.

It is also, ironically, the most difficult basic effect to do. That's because it is the technique, not the tool, that creates the look. Practice—on a scrap piece of wallboard or the closet in a back bedroom—is essential before you tackle your living room wall.

Expect to experiment for a while before you get the hang of this technique. The idea is to create as random a look as possible, and to avoid a columns-and-rows effect by rotating your wrist before you bring the sponge in contact with the wall. That's because unlike manufactured artifacts, natural materials often have a random appearance.

A natural sea sponge is one of the oldest faux finishing tools—and one of the best. Unlike synthetic sponges, each one is unique, imparting a random, highly textured look to your project. They absorb and manipulate glaze well, and they're reusable and incredibly durable: wash and rinse them out and they return to their original shape, ready for the next job.

WHAT TO LOOK FOR

Get at least one good-sized sea sponge. The larger the sponge, the more textural choices you have, as each face of the sponge will offer you different options. Also, the bigger the sponge, the faster your job will go, and the less fatiguing your project will be. While you're at it, pick up a hair clip from a beauty or discount store. The clip's spring-loaded teeth will help you hold onto the sponge, especially when the tool is saturated with slippery glaze. A set of long-handle tongs is a good accessory as well, allowing you to easily reach into corners and the tops of tall walls.

 BASIC. But making the result look random takes practice.

1

SPONGE POSITIVE

The sponge positive technique adds a glaze of a contrasting color to a base coat. Here the base coat is light, the glaze is a couple shades darker. As with all faux techniques, you apply the base coat first and allow it to dry overnight.

> Stop, wash, and rinse out your sponge. Use your second sponge when the tool becomes saturated with glaze to the point that the effect is about to change. How do you know? Practice!

2

2

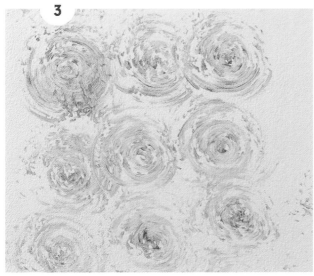

3

1. **Start applying the glaze.** If you're right-handed, work from right to left and from the bottom of the wall up. This method allows you to work at arm's length, reducing fatigue and providing enough distance to see how the effect develops. Since you are more likely to make a mistake early in the job, before you get used to the tool, starting at the bottom keeps any faux pas well below eye level.

2. **Open and close the door.** Tap the wall with the sponge, lift the sponge off the wall surface, then rotate your wrist before tapping the wall again. I call the wrist rotation "opening and closing the door" as it imitates the motion you make when twisting a doorknob. Doing so increases the randomness of the effect, because the sponge hits the wall in a different orientation with each tap. Make sure the sponge is not in contact with the wall when you rotate your wrist, however, or you'll get little tornado-shaped, blurred twist marks on the wall that will disrupt the effect.

3. **Don't create columns and rows.** We're not striving to be accountants here. To avoid creating a linear pattern like this one, work in about a 30-foot square area of the wall at a time, creating an imaginary box, then spiraling in from the edge. When you're done, blend the section into the one next to it.

SPONGE NEGATIVE

The sponge negative effect uses the sponge to manipulate glaze and remove it from the wall—not to apply it, as with sponge positive. To create this technique, have a partner apply the glaze to about 4 feet of wall area while you follow and "sponge off." You really need two people, as you want to sponge off the glaze shortly after it is applied. If too much time intervenes, the glaze will begin to dry, and the effect won't be homogeneous. For that reason, it's best to practice this technique in a room with approximately the same temperature and humidity as the room you plan to finish so you learn just how much working time you have before the glaze starts to set. The sponge negative technique is actually easier to do well than sponge positive, and is more forgiving of mistakes: If you really mess up, you can just reglaze and start again.

1. **Same technique.** Use the same approach as with sponge positive—work from the bottom up, starting with the side of the room that corresponds with your dominant hand. Remember to work in a box, spiral in and blend the effect, rotate your wrist, and change sponges before the effect degrades.

2. **Different results.** The look, however, is strikingly different from sponge positive. Sponge negative leaves more of the glaze on the wall, resulting in a softer, more mottled, less pixilated look.

from rags to richness

Rag-rolling imparts a rich, textured finish fast—and is one of the easiest faux finishes to master.

RAG-ROLLING IS ONE OF THE EASIER FAUX FINISHING EFFECTS to create, and one of the fastest to apply. The reason for both of these attributes is this: unlike sponge painting, which is all about technique, rag-rolling is an effect where you can let the tool do the work and simply enjoy the process.

And the results are great. I describe the finish as a "pseudo leather" look, because the completed effect suggests the softness, the folds, wrinkles, and grain of leather, without specifically trying to reproduce the look, feature for feature, of a real piece of cowhide.

The first rag-rolled effects were created by literally twisting and rolling a piece of fabric into something that looked like a big wrinkled sausage, then rolling it over the wall with bare hands. As you might imagine, this process took forever and was very messy. Some purists still finish walls this way, but when technology can help you do a better job faster, I'm all for it. Like most professional faux finishers, I create this effect by wrapping a twisted rag around a paint roller or by using a special roller of my own design (see the "Tool Profile" sidebar at right).

Once the tool is ready to go, it's just a matter of making several passes over the wall at different angles to create the random effect. The more passes you make, and the more angles you employ, the more subtle and natural your effect will look—so go nuts!

 BASIC. The tool does most of the work for you.

ragging

To complete this effect, you need a rag, a roller, and some rubber bands to attach the rag to the roller. I recommend using a foam roller, because it will even out the pressure on the rag, keeping it in contact with the wall surface at all times. That results in a more even application (or removal) of glaze, and a softer, more abstract, more pleasing effect than a conventional fuzzy roller, which has less "give." You can wrap the roller with all kinds of materials. I describe some of my favorites and the effects they create on page 105.

THE WIZARD'S NEW WAND

To make rag-rolling even easier, I use a commercially made roller with a rag that's permanently stitched on. The result is a more evenly mottled effect, and easier application. You don't need to roll and rubber-band the rag on, or deal with removing it once it's saturated with glaze.

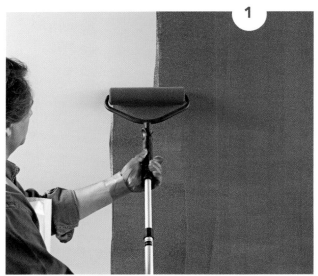

RAG NEGATIVE

As with other faux effects, ragging can be positive or negative: positive adds glaze with the rag roller to a base coat that's applied previously and allowed to dry

Rag-rolling is a bit of a fantasy abstraction—you're not trying to recreate a certain material, so you can be a bit random and carefree in your application. You're trying to create artful chaos.

overnight; negative partially removes glaze from a wall while the glaze is still wet. I prefer the negative effect as it adds a natural, organic quality to a room.

1. Glaze the wall. Glaze about a 4-foot section at a time to ensure that the glaze is still wet when you rag-roll it. Because the rag roller allows you to work fast, you don't need a partner to create this effect, although it goes more smoothly if you do.

2. Rag off. Start by drawing the rag roller diagonally across the wall, maintaining an even pressure and speed. Practice will tell you what works best. Press too hard or roll too fast and the effect degrades— and glaze starts to fly! Even at moderate rolling speeds, you'll want to have other surfaces well masked and covered, since the uneven surface of the rag roller flings the glaze around a bit.

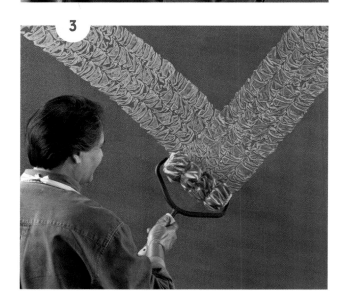

3. Make repeated passes at different angles. Make your second pass at right angles to the first. Notice how the effect becomes much softer and random where the two roller trails overlap. That's what you're after, and the more passes you make at different angles, the more subtle and layered the effect. So roll on, changing angles constantly.

Bubble wrap

Terry cloth

Plastic sheeting

Rag-rolling can produce a tremendous variety of effects because just about anything you can wrap around a paint roller—burlap, lace, plastic, bubble wrap, chamois, terry cloth, old T-shirts, you name it—can be used to absorb or make an impression in the wet glaze. And each material creates a different look. Here are a few of my favorites.

BUBBLE WRAP Ragging allows you to really step out of the box when it comes to tools. Bubble wrap is great stuff—it's got a coarse texture already, so you don't need to twist it when applying it to the roller, which makes prepping the tool easier. Because it's plastic, it won't absorb glaze, but it will displace it. The effect is a bit softer than with an absorbent material, and also allows the roller to be used longer between cleanings, since the glaze doesn't load up nearly as quickly as will fabric. And, when it does come time to clean it, the glaze comes off right away.

TERRY CLOTH Terry is the opposite of bubble wrap: highly absorbent, yet very finely textured. For that reason, I generally give terry a twist when applying it to the roller, and secure it with rubber bands. Unlike bubble wrap, which produces an even effect over the full width of the roller, the terry-covered roller will leave two stripes where the rubber bands depress the cloth and clamp it to the roller. For that reason, you need to make more paths over the surface than with bubble wrap in order to roll out those stripes and create a random, unpatterned surface. The swirling veins left on the surface by twisted terry are a classic ragged look, perhaps most closely approximating leather.

PLASTIC SHEETING Like bubble wrap, plastic sheeting lets you combine a high-tech material with a time-honored technique, expanding your creative options. I like to crinkle and twist the plastic as I apply it to the roller, overlapping several layers of the thin material for more texture. Like bubble wrap, it can be used quite a while before you need to clean the roller, and it, too, displaces rather than absorbs glaze. The result, though, looks surprisingly natural: like the crystal structure in quartz.

striation creation

Combing and dragging are a pair of techniques that are simpler than they look, and they produce great results.

combing and dragging

COMBING AND DRAGGING CAN BE BOLD OR SUBTLE, large scale or small scale, dramatic and contemporary or soft and old-world. No matter what result you're after, you use the same relatively simple technique. What makes the difference is the choice of the tool you use, the color choices you make and, believe it or not, the amount of pressure you apply when you drag the tool down the wall. (Greater pressure, ironically, yields a softer effect.) Combing is a technique for displacing glaze with a comblike tool, such as a rubber squeegee with notches cut in its blade. It produces crisp, bold stripes. Dragging displaces glaze, but it also pulls and blends it at the same time. It produces a softer, less-contrasty effect.

As with many faux techniques, combing and dragging originated in France, where they were invented to emulate the beautiful striped fabrics used as wallcoverings in the homes of the wealthy and called strei, or stripes. Because the results can be so varied and you can work so fast, I've applied combed finishes to ceilings, floors, and furniture as well as walls in just about every type of room you can name. So go nuts! All you're risking is your time and a can of paint. Although the surface looks richly textured, that's all it is—a look. The actual surface is still flat, so you can sand, prime, and repaint a combed finish just as easily as a monochromatic wall.

 BASIC. Varied tools produce a surprizing variety of looks.

Combing and dragging are tool-driven techniques and invite technological experimentation. Traditionally faux finishers dragged a comb, paintbrush, or broom through glaze to produce the effect. We still use those tools today, but now there are several additional options.

THE TRICK'S IN THE TOOL

Wallpaper brushes are great because they have a narrow row of coarse nylon bristles that leave a distinctive texture—plus the brush is 12 inches wide, speeding your work. Rubber window squeegees also make terrific dragging tools, as their blades displace glaze well and can easily be notched to create a variety of scales and patterns. You can even attach long handles to squeegees when working in tall rooms and stairwells. For really dramatic looks in large spaces I like to use a driveway surfacing broom and a squeegee with large-scale notches cut in the blade.

107

UNLIKE OTHER FAUX EFFECTS, combing and dragging involves only simple, one-directional, repetitive motions (later, we'll show you more complex ways to apply this technique). So if you're not comfortable with the random, abstract nature of, say, sponging, combing might be a great place for you to start. Paint your base coat and let it dry overnight. Mix up your glaze, which is typically the same hue as the base coat, but a bit lighter or darker (I used a much more dramatic contrast here so the effect would be easy to see). You can also use white as a base coat, as I have here. As with other faux finishes, you want an eggshell or satin finish for the base. Unlike flat paint, it helps the glaze adhere to the wall without absorbing it, making your job easier.

1. **Roll on the glaze** using the three-stroke, up-down-up method outlined on page 81. Overlap your strokes slightly to maintain a wet edge. To avoid the glaze drying too quickly, limit your work to a 4×8-foot section of wall at a time. If you find your glaze is a bit too dry to work easily by the time you've finished a section, either glaze smaller sections at a time or add just a bit of Floetrol or fabric softener to the glaze to extend working time.

2. **It's a drag!** Take your tool—here I'm using a conventional paintbrush—and drag it straight down the wall from top to bottom. Feel free to experiment with the dragging pressure and angle—notice I'm dragging the length of the bristles down the wall here, not just the tips, for a coarser effect. More pressure also yeilds more constrast.

3. **Use different tools for different effects.** Wallpaper brushes are terrific: their narrow row of coarse bristles gives a wall character and they rinse out quickly and easily. Plus their size allows you to do a foot-wide swipe at a time, reducing the time for larger jobs.

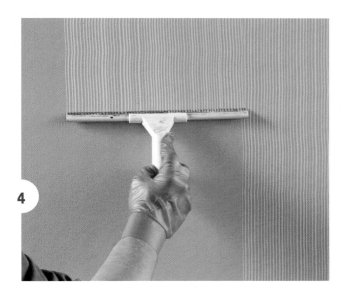

4. Window squeegees are one of my favorite combing tools. The rubber blades displace nearly all the glaze they come in contact with, resulting in sharp, high-contrast lines. Notch little "v" cutouts in the blades with a utility knife or nail clipper to create a comb-like edge. Nibble away at it randomly with a nail clipper for an abstract pattern like this, or ...

5. Keep to the straight and narrow by carefully measuring and marking the rubber edge, then cutting precise, evenly spaced notches in it to create a highly regular striped effect.

6. A trip to the home center store will reveal even more tool options. This squeegee and broom combination is sold to spread and level driveway sealer, but its coarse texture and big scale make it a great combing alternative. I'm using the bristles here, but notching the squeegee side of the tool offers another clever option. Tools such as these that have handles have better ergonomics. Rotate your wrist up when you reach the bottom of your stroke so you can drag all the way to the floor.

3 ways to finish

1 The simplest form of combing involves making a single, top-to-bottom vertical pass down the glazed wall with your tool. This is the fastest way to execute the technique and yields crisp results.

2 Multiple passes through the glaze are a second option. The effect tends to soften with each succeeding pass as the tool marks blend and layer. The result is a bit more subtle and lower in contrast. So if you think one pass looks a bit coarse or stark, take a few more swipes at the wall.

3 Combing again after the glaze partially dries produces a third effect. The glaze moves differently in its partially dried, gel-like state. It can be fun to experiment with recombing the gel at varying degrees of "set" to find which produces the effect you like best.

hit the wall

Flogging is pretty basic: you pick up a brush or mop and give the wall a good whack. It's fun, and results vary widely with tool choice.

FLOGGING IS WHAT I CALL A "PORTAL TECHNIQUE." Once you understand flogging, you understand faux finishing.

I like people to start with this simple technique: Pick up a common household tool like a duster, a mop, or even a lowly toilet cleaning brush and whack it against a wall. If you can do that, you can create a faux finish.

Of course, there's a bit more to it than that, but much faux finishing is about unlearning what we've been taught about painting since kindergarten: Stay within the lines, and don't make a mess.

I say cut loose and have fun! Go ahead—WHACK that wall and see what happens. Whack it every which way—the more randomly the better. And don't worry about precision and detail—at least not with this effect. Flogging is not about detail. It's about creating an overall impression. I actually encourage people to work faster than they think they can, to pick up two tools, one in each hand and have at it. Once you free yourself from the tyranny of your left brain—the logical, tidy, think-inside-the-box side of your head— amazing things can happen. And the things you learn flogging are directly applicable to other faux techniques.

There are other reasons I love this technique. It's fast. It can produce incredibly varied results. And it's a good workout!

BASIC. Simple, physical and fast, flogging is one of my favorites.

flogging

I divide this effect's tools into two categories: flogging tools and whacking tools. Both have long handles for leverage, and for reaching the tops of high walls and into corners.

FLOGGING'S GREATEST HITS

Flogging tools are absorbent. They can either apply or suck up glaze, and include mops, dusters, and other tools that create a random pattern when they hit the wall—a pattern which changes with each strike.

Whacking tools are not absorbent; instead, they displace glaze. These include various types of plastic brushes. I've found that truck tire brushes and toilet cleaning brushes work great, since they're tough, easy to clean, and wonderfully ergonomic.

You use both flogging and whacking tools with the same striking motion, but they make a different sound when hitting the wall—hence the different names. You'll also use application trays, old terry-cloth towels, and the usual masking, application, and cleaning tools and materials.

THINK NEGATIVE

You CAN apply glaze to a wall by flogging or whacking—called a positive effect—but I don't recommend starting with that technique. Taking glaze off—called a negative effect—is easier to do, since you can always take off a bit more, refining the results as you go. If you really screw up, simply reroll the glaze and start again. On the other hand, if you're working on a positive effect and hit a wall too hard, use an overloaded tool, or go over an area too often with a glaze-loaded tool, there's not much you can do to fix your mistake. So to begin with, anyway, think negative!

1. **Apply the glaze.** Just roll it on over a satin or eggshell base coat that has cured overnight. When you're working, keep your tool right in front of your body where you can see it and control it most easily, not off to one side where you have to lean, twist, and strain to use it. I am working off to the side in many of these photos so you can look over my shoulder and see what I'm doing. I usually work with my arms straight in front of me and move across the wall with my whole body as the effect progresses.

2. **Start whacking.** After glazing about a 4×8-foot wall section, pick up a tool or two and start striking the wall. The tools should be clean and moist—wring them out or pat them dry with a terry towel so they are able to absorb the glaze. Using two tools at once allows you to go twice as fast. Here I'm using a couple of tire brushes, but often I'll use different tools in each hand—one with a fine texture, for example, and one with a coarse one—to add depth and variety to the finish.

3. **Varied tools create varied results.** This small car mop creates a randomly mottled effect, which can vary with the thickness of the glaze and the force of the impact with the wall. Generally you want to hit the surface hard enough to create an impression, but not so hard that you wear yourself out after a few blows, or damage the base coat or wall.

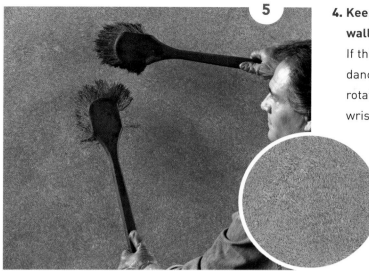

4. Keep the surface of the tool parallel with the wall, but constantly vary the angle it hits the wall. If this photo were a video, you'd see me almost dancing away with my upper body as I flogged, rotating my shoulders, my elbows, and my wrists to make sure the tool didn't hit the wall at the same angle twice. Failing to vary the angle produces a patterned series of impressions—not the random, mottled look we're after.

5. Brushes create a stippled look. The soft, impressionistic result varies with the size of the brush, the arrangement of the bristles, and how many passes you make over a given area.

6. Mops create a mottled look. The soft, random pattern of a dust mop is coarser, but also more muted and less grainy than a brush's stippling. Here, I'm using a large car duster—handy for doing large areas quickly, and creating a larger-scale texture than the smaller mop shown in photo 3.

don't cut corners

One of the things I like about flogging tools—especially car mops and tools with similarly floppy heads—is that they work in corners too. With other effects such as sponging, you often have to resort to smaller-scaled tools to reach into corners, but the individual strands of yarn that these mops are made up with extend outward from the plastic head, reaching right into corners and up to moldings. That means you don't have to change tools as you approach an edge or corner. And that saves you time and makes it easy to preserve the continuity of the effect. A tip: get a feel for how far out from the plastic tool head the yarn extends, so you don't hit the adjacent wall with the solid head of the mop, creating a blur. Remember to mask anything you don't want pigment on, of course.

all washed up?

Washes take a bit of practice to execute—but the soft, subtle, aged effects they create make them a rewarding choice.

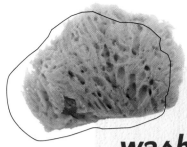

washing

WASHING IS ALL ABOUT TONAL VALUES—creating varying intensities of the same hue. The glazes are applied with a sponge, then partially "washed off" with another sponge, leaving a very soft, ethereal, antiqued look that some people describe as "Tuscan" or "weathered." Unlike some other faux effects, it isn't designed to replicate a particular material. Perhaps for that reason, a wash is a great backdrop: It is better at showcasing furnishings and artwork than more representational effects. Yet it still adds drama and depth, because like other faux effects, it is composed of highlights and shadows.

Washes also suggest antiquity, for several reasons. First, a washed surface looks weathered, as though bleached by the sun and eroded by the wind and rain over the course of time. The finish also replicates the look produced by early, primitive paints, such as whitewash or milk paint, which were fine-grained pigments suspended in water or milk, and resulted in an uneven and somewhat translucent effect as their pigments gradually wore away.

Although they look subtle and primitive, washes are not particularly easy to achieve. First, you're starting with a positive effect, sponging glaze on the wall. Then, you switch to a negative process—sponging glaze back off again, but with a different sponge. Your ultimate aim is to create slight variations in tonal values, and doing so effectively takes practice.

BASIC. The tools are simple, but the effect takes patience to develop.

TOOL PROFILE

Washing is a hand effect and, unlike rag-rolling, there's no technological shortcut to make the job any faster, easier, or better. Since you're literally "washing" pigment onto or off the wall, a good sponge is your primary tool. I usually use a natural sea sponge (with a hair-clip handle—see page 91) for the initial application, and a synthetic tile sponge for blotting and further refining the finish. You'll also need an application tray.

ONE NIGHTSTAND

I use a TV tray—the cheap, stamped-steel kind with metal legs and a nice deep, lipped edge—as a mobile worktable on which to set my sponges and application tray. I cover the tray with several layers of extra-large aluminum foil. When I'm done, I just peel off the aluminum foil, exposing the next layer—no cleaning!

ONE OF THE SECRETS to a good wash finish is how thick to mix the glaze. Use the glaze formula on page 88, but thin it with a bit more water. Exactly how much more is a matter of judgment, like how much flour to add when making gravy. The precise mixture depends on temperature, humidity, surface porosity, and glaze color. Start by adding a cup of water to ten cups of the glaze mixture. Add more—up to one cup per six cups of glaze—if it still seems too thick. Experiment with different mixtures on your practice wall. When you find exactly the right formula for your job, mix up more glaze than you think you'll need. If you run short, your second batch will never match your first, ruining the effect.

1. **Load the sponge.** Fill your application tray about one-third full (too much glaze makes the tray harder to handle, invites spills, and can overload the sponge). Dip the sponge in the tray three times: dippy, dippy, dippy. Then tap the sponge three times on a flat surface to remove any excess: tappy, tappy, tappy. I like to use a roller tray as my applicator tray so I can tap the sponge on the rake of the tray, automatically recycling excess glaze.

2. **Wash the wall with a sea sponge.** Use swirling motions, working on a 3- to 4-foot square of wall at a time. Don't lift the sponge from the wall. Instead imagine you're washing it, not painting it, and gently rub the surface. If the glaze seems a bit hard to work, add a little fabric softener to the mix—not a lot, just a touch—to improve flow. The texture of the sea sponge adds character to the effect.

3. **Blot the wall with a synthetic sponge.** Put down the sea sponge and pick up a synthetic sponge. I use a tile sponge because they're large, very absorbent, and rinse out well. Dampen the sponge, then gently blot the wall to break up the uniformity of the surface and create highlight and shadow.

4. Continue to blot randomly, rotating your wrist to change the aspect angle of the sponge using the "opening and closing the door" motion described on page 100. Don't swirl or twist the sponge when it is in contact with the surface during this step: twist, blot, remove the sponge from the surface, then repeat the sequence.

5. Pull the sponge downward over the surface. Depending on the degree of subtlety you're looking for, the blotted wall may seem a bit blotchy and high-contrast. If that's the case, blend and smooth the surface by pulling a clean, damp tile sponge down the wall as though you're creating a strié effect, which will help even out the tone.

6. Flip the sponge over and continue. When one side of the sponge becomes loaded with glaze, flip it over and continue with the other side. As with sponge finishing, the trick is to know when the sponge is approaching the saturation point where the effect will be degraded, and to flip the sponge BEFORE you reach that point. Exactly when is something you can learn only by practice and careful observation, so just like other faux effects, first experiment on a practice wall. If all else fails, simply wash off your wash completely, wait for the wall to dry, and start again!

experiment

Experiment, but don't go overboard. Working with a wash is like painting with watercolors—you only have so much control. Remember, this effect is about creating an inconsistent surface, so don't try to make it look uniform. Sometimes I even spritz the surface lightly with a water bottle to further dilute the pigment and add to the weathered look. On the other hand, don't fuss with the effect all day. You must know when to walk away, and that's something experience will teach you.

doing denim

Denim, also called chambray, imparts a soft, warm, informal, and comfortable look that puts people right at ease.

CHAMBRAY EMULATES THE SOFT TEXTURE OF WORN FABRIC.
I use this technique quite a bit in informal rooms, such as rumpus rooms, family rooms, playrooms, and kids' bedrooms. Although most often executed in light blue to suggest denim, you can use this effect in a wide variety of colors. Just like the sight of your favorite pair of jeans, this effect creates a visual comfort zone. Here you'll be stacking two effects on top of one another, first dragging down the wall, then across it. The result looks like the warp and woof of loom-woven cloth.

As always, the best way to experiment is on a half-sheet of wallboard. Fasten it to the studs in your garage wall with a few wallboard screws, and experiment to your heart's content. When you think the finish is close to what you'd like, unscrew the wallboard and rest it against a wall in the room you intend to paint. Move it around, placing it against all the surfaces you want to finish. Look at it during different times of the day, in a variety of lights. Once you see it in place, you may find you want to lighten or darken the tone before you attempt the finish on the actual walls.

INTERMEDIATE. Like combing, but in two different directions.

chambray

Technically, this is a variation on a combing technique: First you comb from top to bottom, then you comb horizontally. The result creates the crisscross, warp-and-woof look of woven fabric. The "worn look" or softness of the effect comes from going over the strokes in both directions several times to layer and blur the individual brush marks. Theoretically, you could use just about any brush to do the job. But since you'll be making multiple passes in each of two directions, you have one outstanding choice:

THE WALLPAPER BRUSH

This brush allows you to texture a 12-inch swath with each pass, cleans easily, and can be bought inexpensively at any hardware, wallcovering, or home improvement store. It's also durable: I've been using mine—for both wallpapering and faux finishing—for 25 years, and it's holding up just fine.

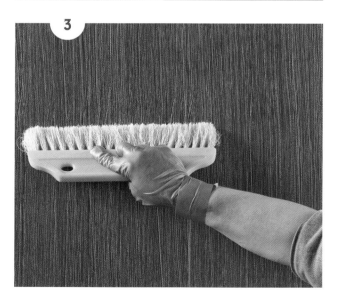

CHAMBRAY AWAY!

The classic choice for a base coat when executing a chambray finish is white; navy blue, of course, is the denim-colored glaze choice. That's because with a white base coat, the more glaze you displace with multiple brush passes, the more the effect takes on the bleached, frayed look of much-worn, much-washed denim clothing. As always, roll on the base coat and let it dry overnight.

1. **Roll on the glaze** covering about a 4×8-foot section of wall at a time. Overlap your strokes to maintain a wet edge, and don't use too much pressure on the roller, which can form little ridges of paint, called "snail trails" in the surface. The smoother the glaze coat, the more even the effect.

2. **Comb the glaze vertically,** pulling the wallpaper brush straight down the wall from top to bottom in one smooth, even, fairly quick motion. If you move the brush too slowly, you're more likely to introduce irregularities and wavy lines in the finish. Plus, it takes longer!

3. **Comb through the glaze again and again.** Make three to five passes to produce a soft effect. Again, move from the top of the wall to the bottom in one motion, and maintain an even pressure on the bristles. Try to keep your strokes as close to true vertical as possible: since we're replicating machine-woven cloth, not the randomness of nature, use straight, parallel strokes.

it takes two

It takes two people to paint a room: one to cut in a corner and out about four feet, and another to brush or roll the paint along the cut-in edge. The two continue working around the room in this manner. One person can paint a room, but it takes longer. It's also harder to keep a wet paint edge.

4. Now comb horizontally. Again, use long, parallel strokes with the wallpaper brush. Maintain even pressure and use a a quick, smooth motion just as you did when dragging the brush down the wall. Don't worry if the glaze starts to gel a bit as you work—that will actually soften the look even more, which suits a chambray finish just fine. As you continue to drag, you'll start to see dibbles—areas where more than the usual amount of glaze has been displaced. These dibbles appear randomly and create white streaks that imitate the textural variations often seen in cotton fabric. You can see one dibble directly below the wallpaper brush in the photo at left.

my mistake!

A SURE CURE FOR ARROGANCE

Everyone hates the preparation you need to go through before you paint a room. Pros like me hate it even more than you do, because we have to do it over and over again. And the truth is, much of the time we could get away without doing it. When you paint every day, you get pretty good, and the drop cloths, the masking tape, and all the rest are like the big net underneath the tightrope walker: a measure of safety that you rarely have to use. But going without can be disastrous.

After a while my skills went to my head. They got the better of my wisdom. I got arrogant. "I'm a pro," I thought. "I don't need to put a drop cloth on the entire floor when I'm just doing one wall. I'll just put a four-foot strip down the edge of the room and save some time."

That was the day, of course, that I spilled an entire quart can of bright red paint. At the moment it happened, I would have gladly exchanged that paint for a quart of my own

blood, as long as I could have spilled the blood anywhere but on my client's brand-new, formerly blinding-white wall-to-wall carpet.

In this case, disaster was averted because my other safety systems were in place: I had color-coded buckets right there filled with my fabric-softener-and-water cleanup solution. I immediately flooded the spill with the solution, then sucked it up with a wet-or-dry shop vac I always keep on hand. To the homeowner's amazement and my considerable relief I got every bit of the stain out. That saved me the $2,000 it would have cost to replace and install a new carpet.

Lesson learned: Don't skimp on the preparation. I immediately went back to the practice of covering the entire floor of any room I'm working in. I still hate it. But now I do it with a smile, knowing that I'll never again have to look at the expression on my client's face when she saw what I'd done to her new carpet.

Better Homes and Gardens.new garden book

really rustic

Here's a fast, easy way to create a finish that looks like it's been around forever.

A RUSTIC FINISH CREATES A DAPPLED BACKGROUND that emulates weathering and suggests age and permanence. I like to use this technique in entryways, as it imparts a feeling of warmth and stability that makes guests feel at home.

I also like this finish because it's fast and easy: The technique is virtually goof-proof. Basically you're creating large blotches of two or more similar colors—those that have the same hue—on the wall. Then you blend these randomly-shaped areas of color (I call them "cow patches") together until they create a subtle, slightly mottled background.

There is a bit of judgment involving color choice, degree of contrast between the color glazes you apply, and how large to scale the cow patches. There are no hard and fast rules about these matters, and the choices you make will depend on the size of the room, the degree of drama you want, and your personal taste. As always, the way to develop this judgment is through practice. A final piece of good news: You can further refine this effect after it dries if you'd like.

 INTERMEDIATE. The technique's easy; the judgement takes practice.

rustic

Aside from a conventional paint roller, you really only need three tools to create a rustic finish: a couple of hot dog rollers, a tile sponge, and a terry-cloth rag.

HOT DOG! WE'RE ROLLIN'

Hot dog rollers, also called European rollers or, inaccurately, trim rollers, are small paint rollers about 4 inches long and a couple inches around. The rollers themselves are generally made of foam and are gently rounded at both ends. These are great tools: they're light, maneuverable, and easy to use. They're perfect for getting in to corners and painting things like cabinets and doors faster and more evenly than a brush. Their job in executing the rustic finish is to apply and blend together the cow patches of colored glaze.

The tile sponge's job is to gently blot the surface, further blending and refining it. And the terry rag? It's what you use to make sure the sponge is not too moist to create the desired effect.

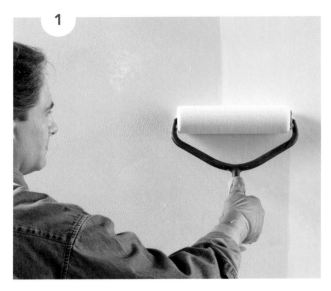

First roll on a satin or eggshell base coat and allow it to dry overnight. And you might not need to paint the whole room. This effect is so abstract and random that sometimes just one or two accent walls is enough, especially if those walls act as background to antique furniture, old photographs, paintings, or memorabilia. On the other hand, there's nothing wrong with using this technique on all four walls, so long as you realize the result will have a strong presence.

1. **Roll on a clear glaze.** After the base coat is dry, mix up the glaze formula on page 88, but omit the pigment. Then apply the glaze to about a 4×8-foot section of wall. This clear layer has several purposes: first, it extends the drying time of the glazes you'll add in Step 2, giving you more time to create the effect. Second, the clear glaze softens and diffuses the colored glazes, making the mixing of colors and the transition from one tone to another more gradual and pleasing.

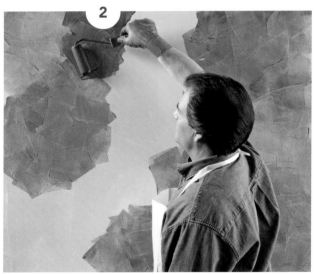

2. **Make the cow patches.** Now take two glaze mixtures of the same hue, or color family. (In this example I'm using mocha and burnt sienna.) Using a different hot dog roller for each color, create 3–6 cow patches of color—large, random-shaped blotches—on your 4×8-foot section of wall. The larger the room and the less contrast in the glaze colors, the larger you can make the blotches.

3. **Blend the patches together.** Using the same hot dog roller, blend the patches together by rolling over and between them with random strokes from a variety of angles. The roller will lift, mix, and redistribute the glaze until the two colors randomly intermix and blend.

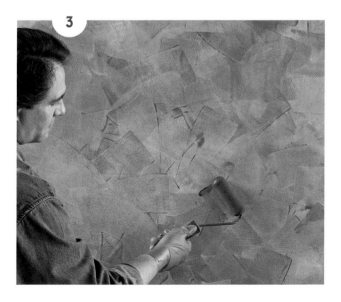

4. Prepare to blot! You can stop after Step 3 if you like, but if you want an even softer effect, dampen, then wring out a tile sponge. To ensure that the sponge isn't dripping, which can cause streaks in your finish, wrap it in a terry-cloth rag and wring it out again.

5. Gently blot the surface, concentrating on darker areas that you'd like to subtly lighten. You'll find the sponge gives you more control lifting the finish than a roller, allowing you to fine-tune the effect.

6. Drag the sponge lightly down the wall, if you like, for a result that's softer yet. Don't overdo it, or your effect will look softer and have less contrast as it dries. And remember, you can always touch it up later, adding either highlights or shadows after the first application dries.

rustic relief

Venetian plaster finishes are all the rage these days, but they're very time-consuming to create. Here's a shortcut that gives you a very similar effect, for dramatically less time and money. First trowel on a standard, premixed drywall compound to the wall with an 8- or 12-inch drywall knife. Apply the compound with random strokes, creating as much or as little texture as you like, as shown below.

After the compound dries, follow the steps above to create the dappled surface color. Once you've finished with the hot dog roller, blot the wall with a terry towel or sponge. You'll find the colored glazes will settle into the crevices and low spots in the textured finish and wick off the high spots, giving your wall an even greater rustic character.

yikes! stripes!

Now it's time to get graphic, with a geometric technique that can help you make everything from a subtle backdrop to a bold statement.

STRIPES AND OTHER GEOMETRIC PATTERNS are unlike the styles we've presented up to this point. Instead of being random and natural looking, they're regular, precise, and graphic. And while most naturalistic faux effects are either tool- or technique-driven, stripes and other geometrics are process-driven.

That doesn't make them easier or more difficult than the other effects—just different. Doing geometrics well requires patience and a bit of math, but other than that, they use the same tools and techniques as other faux finishes.

In return, the finishes are so dramatic and powerful that you'd have to hire an architect and contractor to achieve results of similar magnitude. Yet the changes are as inexpensive as a can of paint and as personal as you want to make them.

I use stripes, in particular, to either camouflage architectural features that I don't like or to emphasize those that I do. For instance, if a low ceiling makes a room seem cramped, I like to visually raise it with a wall of relatively narrow stripes. If a stairwell seems broken up by all the angles: the risers, the landings, the railing, the turns—I like to use subtle, tone-on-tone stripes to give it a bit of visual coherence. And if a room has some existing architecture that deserves more play, such as columns or balusters, I might emphasize those features with complementary stripes on the wall.

> **INTERMEDIATE.** The layout's the challenge; the painting goes fast.

TOOL PROFILE

stripes

One tool you'll use LOTS of when painting stripes is masking tape—rolls and rolls of it! I like to use 2-inch tape in multiple widths to create larger stripes: three slightly overlapping applications, for instance, to mask off a 5-inch stripe. For stripes much wider than that, use plastic wrap, cut to just under the width you want to mask. Secure it to the wall on each side with tape. It's great stuff, and can save time and money if you're creating, say, 8-inch stripes.

STRAIGHT AND NARROW

The other tools you'll need include a tape measure to lay out the stripes on the wall, and a 4-foot carpenter's level to make sure the stripes are plumb and to use as a straightedge to mark the stripes on the wall before masking. Finally you'll want a white chalk pencil to make your layout marks. Regular graphite pencils smudge and stain when used on paint. Chalk pencils produce softer marks that are easy to remove and won't stain your finish.

127

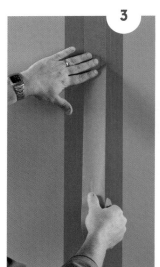

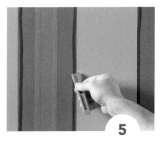

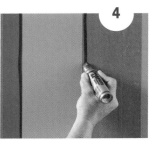

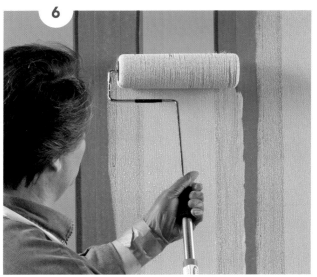

THE KEY TO STRIPES and other geometric effects is patient preparation. If you measure, lay out, and mask with care, your job is essentially done by the time you open a paint can. As dramatic as stripes are, there's very little technique to the actual painting.

1. **Once you've determined the exact width** of your stripes, mark the location of each stripe on the wall. Use a tape measure at eye level, and mark the stripe locations with a white chalk pencil.

2. **Lay out the stripes** using a carpenter's level. Position the level at each tick mark you made on the wall, then use it to determine a plumb line. Mark the line with your white chalk pencil, making sure to hold the pencil at the same angle to the level each time to avoid wavy lines or variations in the width of the stripes. Mark each section of wall that is to be covered with tape with a light "X."

3. **Tape off** the wall sections marked with an X. Overlap tape when covering wall sections more than a single tape-width wide. For really wide stripes of 6 inches or more in width, cut plastic wrap slightly less than the width of the stripe you desire, then seal it to the wall with masking tape. This saves time, tape, and money.

4. **Mark the outside edges of the tape** with a magic marker. While not critical when you've taped off the whole stripe, as I have here, it indicates which side of the tape on which to paint when your stripes are wider and you don't mask off the whole stripe.

5. **Seal the tape** by running a burnisher quickly down the edge of the tape to prevent paint from leaking underneath (see page 69 for more information).

6. **Roll on the paint.** Use the three-stroke application rule outlined on page 81. Here's where the time spent masking really pays off!

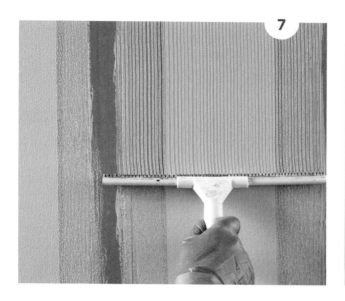

7. Add a strié. You can stop after Step 6, if you like, and I often do myself. If you want a somewhat more dimensional and sophisticated effect, you can add a strié to your stripe, layering your effect with texture. Just drag a notched squeegee, a brush, or another dragging tool (see page 107 for more information) down the wall while the paint is still wet.

8. Pull the tape 60 minutes after you apply the finish. The finish will have started to dry, so it won't run, but won't have hardened yet, so it will shear cleanly along the tape line. If you wait until the paint dries, the finish is more likely to fracture irregularly, ruining the effect. Also, pull the tape straight down, as shown. Pulling down, not out, lessens the chance that you'll pull the base coat—or even pieces of plaster or wallboard paper—off the wall.

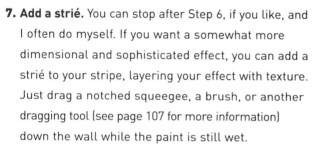

zebra math

Relax—we're not talking calculus, just simple division. But determining correctly and exactly how wide your stripes should be is what makes the difference between a crisp, professional-looking job and an amateurish one. Measure the length of the focal point wall—the wall across from the room's main entry door—in inches. Then divide that number by the width of stripes you desire. For instance, a 144-inch wall divided by 8-inch stripes equals 18 stripes. If the wall isn't evenly divisible by the number of inches in the width of the stripe you desire, modify the stripe width slightly until a given number of stripes fills each wall exactly. For instance, if the length of the wall was 150 inches, divide 150 by the 18 stripes you desire. The result in this case is 8⅓ inches, so that's the width of stripe to create. Do the same with all the other walls, modifying the stripe width slightly for each as required so the stripes fit each wall evenly. Your eye won't be able to tell the difference in stripe width but will notice the even fit.

multihue wash

Subtle splashes of contrasting colors add an ethereal, impressionistic vibrancy to a room.

LOOK AT THE WALL on the opposite page. What do you see? Bold color? Certainly not. In fact, you may not have realized right away that you weren't looking at a monochromatic wall. But look again, and you'll see very subtle splashes of color—almost as though you were looking at a landscape through a bright mist or haze. Colors seem to float in the mist, to fade in and out—one hue becoming more prominent, then another.

I call this multicolor, soft, floating, ethereal effect a "multihue wash." It creates an almost surrealistic, postmodern look. Gazing at such a wall, it's almost as though you look past the literal effect and get a subconscious sense of how the colors blend and flow. This effect is great for bringing out accent colors in a room. It also works well as a foil for high-gloss, high-contrast furnishing, such as modern chrome and leather sofas.

As with other more advanced effects, a multihue wash works best as an accent wall in a special area such as an entry, dining room, or game room. In the photo opposite, the effect lends a shimmering, misty-rainbow backdrop to a display of an exotic—but solid, hard and shiny—piece of carved stone sculpture. It's almost as though there's an out-of-focus, misty, faraway landscape out there that adds to the mystery of this artifact from a distant culture.

INTERMEDIATE. A good introduction to stacking and blending.

multihue wash

For this technique, you need only three types of tools.

ROLL, ROLL, AND RAG

First you need a conventional roller to apply the background color and, later, a clear glaze. Second, you'll need as many 4-inch long "hot dog" rollers and roller frames as there are glaze colors in your effect. These rollers have medium-density foam covers that come to a rounded end. (You'll be laying down several colors and won't have time to stop, clean, and reuse one roller for each hue.)

I also like to go to the supermarket and get several aluminum baking pans with snap-on plastic covers, one for each glaze color. Get large enough pans so you can lay the hot dog roller down in the pan and snap on the lid for airtight storage.

Finally, you'll need a terry rag to blot off the finish when you're done, adding a little texture to the effect.

131

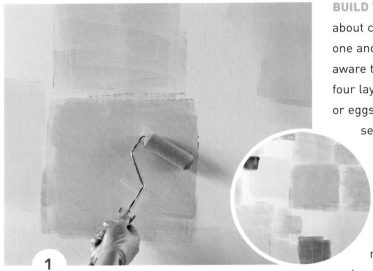

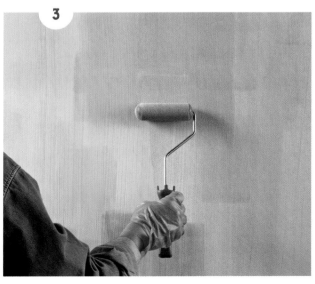

BUILD THE EFFECT WITH LAYERS. Block wash is all about creating splashes of color that contrast with one another—but so softly and subtly, you're barely aware that they exist. To create this effect, we work in four layers. First, the background color, a semigloss or eggshell paint is rolled on and allowed to cure. The second layer—although you can't see it in these photos, because it is colorless—is a generous coat of clear glaze. I like to extend the glaze's working time a bit by adding a little extra Floetrol or fabric softener to the mix (see page 88). That's layer two. The numbered photos pick up the process after the clear glaze is applied.

1. **Roll on the patches of color.** To create patches that have a pleasing size relationship to one another and to the wall on which they're applied, start by creating some large patches that are approximately a quarter the size of the dimensions of the wall. Then, mix in four more sizes of patches, each half the size of the next larger patch. So, for instance, the patch sizes for an 8×8 foot wall would be approximately 2 feet square, one foot square, six inches square, and three inches square. Start by putting down the largest size patches, then move down to the next size and so on. Don't paint all the patches of one size all the same color, either. You're aiming for an even distribution of sizes and colors, but no obvious pattern. Try to put patches of contrasting color next to one another so they stand out a bit. And leave a bit of "white space" between each block. The amount of space will vary somewhat from patch to patch, and that's fine. The more random and splotchy, the better. Since you're laying down colored glazes on top of a still-wet clear glaze, the hues will lighten and disperse a bit on application. That's exactly what you want to happen.

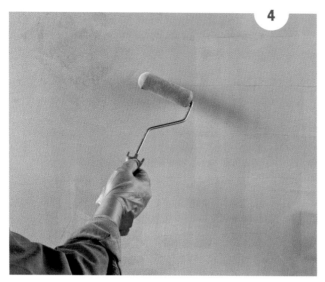

2. Now add another layer of clear glaze. Once you've rolled on patches of various colors and sizes, roll on another coat of clear glaze with a conventional roller. This will further diffuse and mix the colors, picking up glaze from one patch and imprinting it on a patch of a different color, or on the white space between patches. Right before your eyes, you'll see the effect becoming softer, more diffuse and more subtle.

3. Blend the blocks. Now pick up a hot dog roller and more clear glaze and work on smaller sections of wall, rolling over the blocks in random directions to blend and overlap their colors.

4. Keep blending until the colors are so subtle and intermixed that you can barely sense where one ends and another begins. Step away from the wall periodically to judge the overall effect and the evenness of the blending.

5. Blot the wall with a damp, clean, scrunched-up terry towel to add some random texture and the appearance of greater depth to the effect.

wizards work wet

"Wet Paint" are two words that strike terror in the hearts of many DIYers—but fluid is your friend.

Can't wait for the paint to dry? You're not alone. Most folks want to get through the messy wet paint stage as fast as possible. Dry paint is tame paint. It stays put. It doesn't drip, run, spatter, or spill. It doesn't end up on your clothes, in your hair, or all over the cat.

Wizards Work Wet. Paint's fluidity is the key to creating magical effects in which colors blend, abstract shapes take form, and highlight, shadow, and depth appear.

Extend your working time. The key to developing and controlling such magic is to work wet—dampen your tools before using them, so they don't "lock on" to the pigments you're working with and refuse to let them go. Extend the drying time of glazes and paints by adding an extending agent such as Floetrol or fabric softener to them when you need extra time to manipulate the pigments. Use coats of clear glaze underneath and on top of pigmented glaze to give the pigments added depth and fluidity.

look—leather!

Soft, sensual, and organic, leather is perhaps the most touchable, approachable effect of all. Difficult? Not really!

LEATHER ADDS A RICH, SENSUAL LOOK to a space. It also implies durability, luxury, strength, and antiquity. It's a great effect to use in a library, study, office, under a chair rail in a dining room, or as an accent wall in a bedroom or family room. Even though it's flat paint on a hard wall, looking at it gives you the feeling of comfort, as though you could sink into it. Leather is also great as a supporting effect for a room: libraries or studies with an English club look are one popular theme; so is a western look.

As luxurious as it appears, leather is just as easy to execute as any other medium-difficulty faux finish. That's because the tools do most of the work. In fact, to make sure I don't "overthink" this technique, I often close my eyes as I work on this effect, helping to ensure that I work as randomly as possible.

We're not trying to duplicate the look of an actual piece of leather, so the effect is more impressionistic than literal. Still, it can be incredibly convincing. On the following pages, I offer two slightly different techniques. The first replicates the look of richly dyed leather, the second, a more organic, naturally tanned skin.

INTERMEDIATE. A bit abstract, but not all that difficult.

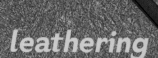

leathering

The tools involved in leathering are common, few, and simple.

RAW HIDE

The primary tool is a conventional roller frame and foam roller, covered with a piece of common plastic wrap. Go around the roller several times, using a diagonal, twisting motion to induce a lot of irregular wrinkling and crinkling—that's what creates the textured look of tanned cowhide. The foam roller cover applies even pressure to the plastic, making it easier to roll and giving you a more uniform effect. You'll also need a terry rag to wipe off the roller occasionally when it becomes overloaded with glaze.

To introduce veins of color, grab a 4-inch-wide hot dog roller. You'll use this in a rather unconventional manner I'll describe later.

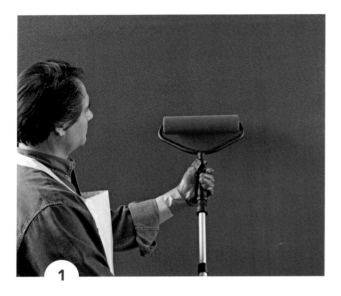

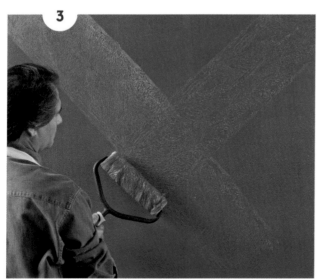

look, use the following technique. It creates a soft, somewhat worn appearance. Think "leather library seat" and you'll come close to the image we're trying to mimic. This is a negative effect, which means you'll be manipulating glaze once it's on the wall to create the look, rather than developing the effect AS you apply the glaze. The first steps of the process are straightforward and by now familiar: apply your background color in a satin or eggshell finish and allow it to dry overnight.

1. **Apply burnt sienna glaze,** covering about a 4×8-foot section of the wall at a time. Better yet, have a partner roll on the glaze so you can follow behind, forming the texture while the glaze is still nice and wet.

2. **Create the texture.** Pick up your plastic-wrapped roller (I've used red-tinted wrap here to help you see the wrapping texture; normally I use clear wrap). Start with a diagonal downward stroke. You'll notice the roller doesn't absorb the glaze, although some will stick to the crevices and wrinkles in the plastic. Mostly it displaces the glaze, stamping it with an impression of the roller's surface texture. I like to use a double-yoke roller handle because it allows me to apply pressure to the roller more evenly, avoiding a linear, patterned effect. What we're after, as usual, is randomness.

3. **Roll again and again.** Go over every section of the wall several times, always from a different angle. The more passes you make over a given spot, the softer and more random the effect. (Although these still photos make my progress look slow and deliberate, I'm actually moving quite quickly, almost dancing in front of the wall, constantly changing the angle I roll.) Remove the roller from contact with the wall when changing angles at the end of each stroke to avoid a smear.

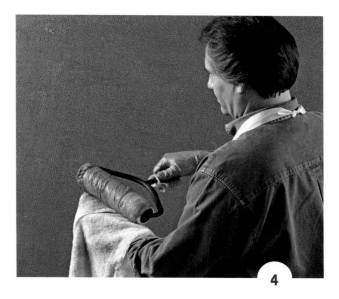

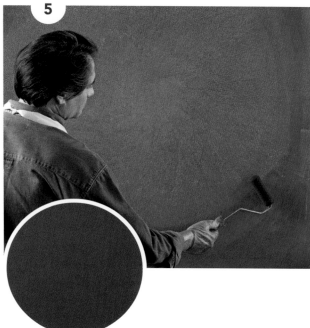

4. Clean the roller occasionally with a terry-cloth towel. The optimum time to do this is right before the roller becomes so slick with glaze that the effect starts to degrade. Practice will quickly tell you when you've reached that point. Meanwhile, if you see the effect change, just pad off the roller and go over that area again.

5. Darken the edges by rolling on a bit of raw umber glaze to the perimeter of the technique with a hot dog roller. Round off the corners, as shown in Step 4, and gradually blend the darker color into the lighter one as you go. This mimics the look of a worn padded surface.

my mistake!

TAKE MY BREATH AWAY

One time many years ago, before I understood the amount of toxins present in the chemicals we handle when we paint, experience offered me a dramatic illustration. One of my assistants keeled over in a dead faint, paintbrush in hand. It turns out he'd been overcome by the fumes present in an alcohol-based stain-killing primer we were using. (Avoiding such fumes is one of the reasons I use water-based paints and glazes whenever I can.) Fortunately, he promptly revived when we moved him outdoors and into fresh air.

Now I know that you don't have to pass out to get hurt by chemical fumes—long-term exposure to toxins in some painting products can create

permanent pulmonary, respiratory, and cognitive problems. You don't normally think of home decorating as a high-risk activity, but if you don't follow the product directions, it can be. In this case, we weren't ventilating the room properly. That allowed fumes to build up.

Lesson learned: Even when using water-based finishes, always open windows and doors for cross-ventilation, and place two large box fans in opposite windows, one blowing fresh air into the room, and one blowing fume-filled air out. Not only will the room be much safer and healthier to work in, it'll smell a lot better, and the paint will dry more evenly.

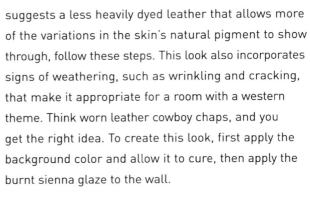

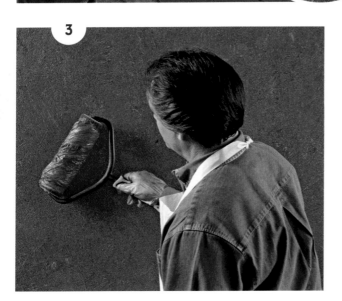

FOR A MORE ORGANIC LEATHER LOOK—one that suggests a less heavily dyed leather that allows more of the variations in the skin's natural pigment to show through, follow these steps. This look also incorporates signs of weathering, such as wrinkling and cracking, that make it appropriate for a room with a western theme. Think worn leather cowboy chaps, and you get the right idea. To create this look, first apply the background color and allow it to cure, then apply the burnt sienna glaze to the wall.

1. **Load a hot dog roller with raw umber glaze.** Raw umber is slightly darker than burnt sienna. Hold the hot dog roller at about a 30–45-degree angle to the wall surface. Put the rounded end of the roller in contact with the wall. Then move the roller down the wall in a random, squiggly motion as shown. The movement combines dragging, twisting, and rolling, and leaves an uneven multitoned smear on the surface. The mark is dark at one edge where the hot dog roller applied some of the raw umber glaze, and lighter on the other side where it lifted some of the of the burnt sienna glaze, allowing the background wall color to peek through. The idea is to infuse a vein of color into the glazed wall.

2. **Apply the texture.** Take the plastic-wrapped conventional roller and make multiple passes at random angles over the wall. This creates visual texture and also blends and churns the two colors of glaze, resulting in a gently mottled effect, reminiscent of the pigment variations in a piece of natural, undyed leather.

3. **Keep going!** Up to a certain point, the more passes, and the more random the passes, the better. For this effect, let the glaze start to gel, and then roll it some more. The gelled glaze gets sticky, and the texture becomes a little more pronounced. Don't roll the glazes all day, though, or they'll become so mixed that you'll have a one-color wall.

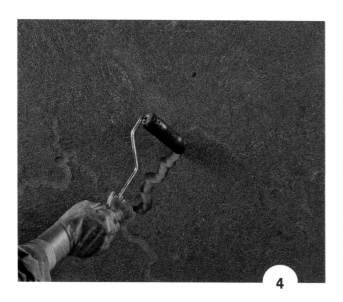

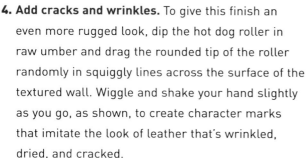

4. Add cracks and wrinkles. To give this finish an even more rugged look, dip the hot dog roller in raw umber and drag the rounded tip of the roller randomly in squiggly lines across the surface of the textured wall. Wiggle and shake your hand slightly as you go, as shown, to create character marks that imitate the look of leather that's wrinkled, dried, and cracked.

5. Blend in the cracks with more random passes of the texture roller. Experience will tell you when to stop. If you overwork this stage, you'll erase the character marks. My mantra for this stage is step away from the wall and look at the overall effect. If you think you're done, stop. Don't second-guess yourself. Your first reaction is usually accurate.

Pet protection

Pets are great, God bless 'em. We love having them around—which is why you should banish them to another room, a friend's house, the fenced yard, or even the boarding kennel, if you have to, while you're working on a faux effect. Think about the consequences of your golden retriever giving you an exuberant greeting while you've got a tray of glaze in one hand and a glaze-loaded sponge in the other. It's not a pretty scene. It won't improve your mood or your décor. More importantly, it could harm your pet. Some dogs will lap up anything, with potentially disastrous effects, and even a cat that inadvertently brushes against wet paint or glaze could poison themselves when they try to lick the paint off their fur. And fumes from various paints and glazes can be far more toxic to some animals than they are to humans. So play it safe, and arrange for your pets to play elsewhere while you work. Of course it goes without saying that young children should never be present while painting is taking place, and should remain elsewhere until the job is done, the tools and materials are cleaned up, the waste disposed of, and the paint dry and room air clean and fit to breathe.

The sky's the limit!

A skyscape filled with puffy white cumulus can be part of your day no matter what the weather. So let the light shine in.

"I'VE LOOKED AT CLOUDS FROM BOTH SIDES NOW," sang Judy Collins. Now you can look at them indoors if you paint them on your bedroom wall. Clouds are a great way to create an outdoor vista and add a bit of whimsey and volume to a space, and a sense of peacefulness and serenity. They're also a wonderful way to support a transportation theme in a kid's bedroom (see page 32 for an example).

Clouds is a complex effect because it combine several different techniques. It also takes a bit of an artistic eye and the ability to create a realistic look. And, you're painting a subject everyone sees every day in nature, so they have a reference point to compare your efforts to. For these reasons, I'd suggest starting with one of the simpler examples and working your way up to this technique.

Done correctly, though, there's nothing that can transform a room—or lift your spirits—quite like a cloudscape. Talk about creating a sense of depth! This faux vista goes on for miles and miles.

ADVANCED. Combines several techniques; a good eye helps.

TOOL PROFILE

clouds

You'll need an eclectic—but not particularly exotic—collection of tools to paint clouds. That's because you're creating both a fairly solid background and a highly textured, wispy-looking subject that requires a lot of manipulation and handwork.

CLOUD KIT

You'll need a conventional wall roller frame and segmented foam cover, along with a roller tray and extension handle to lay down the base coat. Also purchase a white chalk pencil to mark the locations of the clouds on the wall. Use chalk because any stray marks will wipe off easily, and the remaining marks literally "paint out" when you apply the pigmented glaze that forms the cloud. A sea sponge, hot dog roller, masonry brush, dishwasher's bottle mop, and tile sponge all come in handy to coax the white glaze into cloudlike forms.

141

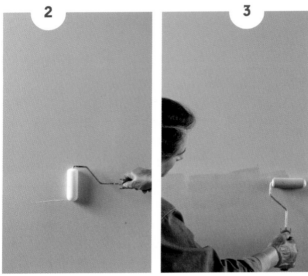

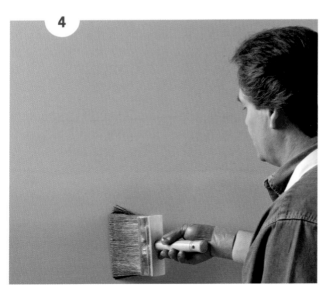

CLOUDING YOUR VISION

Creating clouds is neither a completely random effect such as pure sponging or flogging, nor a highly precise geometrical layout such as stripes or diamonds. It combines both skills: clouds need to appear randomly placed to look like a real skyscape, yet properly oriented toward the viewer to suggest a realistic perspective and a natural sun position and wind direction. Begin by painting the walls a medium-blue base coat in a satin or eggshell finish and allowing the paint to dry overnight.

1. **Put a pencil to it.** Take a white chalk pencil and lightly draw in the bottoms of the clouds on the wall. Cloud bottoms are the easiest parts to start with because they usually appear flat. Position some large clouds fairly far apart to create a foreground; add medium cloud shapes a bit closer to each other to form the midground; and cluster small clouds even closer together to form the background. The clouds should naturally recede into the distance, as they reach toward the horizon.

2. **Create a horizon.** Roll clear glaze onto the bottom third of the wall with a hot dog roller in about 3×4-foot sections.

3. **Darken the horizon.** Then roll blue paint that's a shade or two darker than the wall into the glaze, blending it in so the darkest blue is at the bottom. The color should fade gradually over the bottom third of the wall until it matches the base color of the top two-thirds.

4. **Blend the horizon in horizontally,** using side-to-side strokes with a masonry brush. The result is quite subtle, and designed to suggest the stratified layers of air and the different temperatures and densities that form the earth's atmosphere.

5. Bring on the clouds. Dip a sea sponge into a tray of white glaze three times: "dippy, dippy, dippy." Then tap the sponge three times on the dry rake of the tray: "tappy, tappy, tappy." When you're done, the sponge should be lightly damp with glaze, not dripping wet. You don't want to glob on the color: you want a translucent effect with a bit of the blue background peeking through. Gently tap the wall, rotating your wrist between taps so the sponge hits the wall at a different orientation with each tap. Start at the bottom of a cloud that's at eye level and build up toward the puffy top of the cloud.

6. Add companion clouds, following your chalk-penciled layout, building clouds of appropriate sizes above each penciled line.

7. Soften the sponge impressions by flogging each cloud gently with a slightly dampened dish mop such as those used to clean the inside of glass tumblers. The yarnlike texture of the mop's head will "smudge down" and break up the crispness of the sponge's impressions. Step back frequently, both to give yourself a midroom view of the cloud you're working on and to see how it fits into the overall composition. Your clouds, like real ones, should be slightly different from each other, yet similar enough to look created by one weather system. Fair-weather cumulus clouds are generally most pleasing. Thunderheads are more dramatic, but do you really want an impending storm on your wall?

MOVE WITH IT!
I like to keep all my tools and materials with me as I work around the room, so I lay them out on a standard card table. I set each table leg on a piano dolly, available from hardware or home center stores. Now you can wheel the table with you as you work.

WEATHER OR NOT TO PAINT
Paint goes on best when there is low humidity and moderate temperatures. If you have to paint in less-than ideal conditions, use paint conditioner as described on page 71, and either a humidifier or a dehumidifier, depending on conditions.

8. **Blot and dab** the surfaces of your clouds with a slightly dampened tile sponge to further soften their texture and give an illusion of depth. Here I'm working on a cloud in the relative background, so it deliberately shows very little detail, as though you were looking at it through several miles of atmospheric haze. Clouds in the foreground are larger and have more texture and detail. Again, step back frequently to view the cloud you're working on in the context of the whole wall.

9. **Add a shadow line.** Often a blue streak defines the bottom of a cloud, where more moisture and denser air combine to give it a more solid appearance than the puffy white top. Take a hot dog roller dampened with some of the darker blue paint you used earlier to create the horizon and drag just the rounded end of the roller across the cloud near the bottom of its form. Don't roll, drag and wiggle, leaving a somewhat uneven streak.

10. **Blend in the streak** by tapping it lightly with the bristle tips on your masonry brush. This time, the masonry brush should be dry: you don't want to absorb the blue paint, just move it around and blend it in a bit. If that lightens the bottom of the cloud too much, drag the hot dog roller again, then tap and blend with the brush.

11. **Add some highlights and even them out.** Roll and drag in highlights with white glaze on a hot dog roller to create the sunstruck tops of your clouds. Then use the bristle tips of a dry masonry brush to even out the effect, blending the white highlights back into the more shadowed and translucent middle of the cloud.

12. **Create the windblown whisps** that characterize cumulus clouds by dragging your masonry brush sideways across the bottom of the cloud. Use the sides as well as the tops of the bristles to avoid an overly striated effect. And always drag in the same direction (I'm going from left to right here) to give a realistic impression of wind direction.

my mistake!

NOT FAUX ENOUGH

Can a faux finish look TOO dramatic? You bet, so it's important for you and whoever else will be inhabiting the space you're painting to agree on what you want. Here's how I found out:

One of my clients had a lot of money and excellent taste and loved his wife very much. He wanted to surprise her with a birthday present: a light, airy, calming bedroom in their master suite. "Paint a cloudscape," he said. "Do the walls, the ceiling, everything." Then he and his wife left for a two-week vacation.

We moved out all the furniture and did one of my favorite jobs of all time. The floor was dark blue, and we painted a gradient of blue that flowed up the walls, over all the architectural detailing, and onto the ceiling. Then we added clouds—beautiful, puffy cumulous. They were gorgeous and, combined with the gradient-painted blue "sky," incredibly realistic.

The couple came back, and the husband walked his wife into the room with her eyes closed. He was delighted with the job and wanted her to experience the full effect. Well, the poor woman opened her eyes and saw clouds. She thought she was looking straight up, but she was in fact looking at the wall. She became so spatially disoriented that she literally toppled over. As you might imagine, I got a phone call. We came back and modified the effect, adding a prominent, white-painted chair rail to serve as a horizon line, with wainscot of a different color below so the woman could enter the room without feeling like she was skydiving.

Lesson Learned: Be careful with bold visual surprises. What you may consider beautiful and calming may create the feeling of free-fall-induced panic in someone else!

wood you?

Now you can have richly paneled walls, moldings, or built-in furniture
that look like an expensive display wood—at a fraction of the cost!

WOODGRAINING IS FAUX FINISHING in a less abstract, more realistic mode. It uses paint, glaze, and technique to make a surface look like a more expensive material. In this case, the goal is to recreate the look of oak paneling.

Woodgraining is most appropriate when used in support of country or traditional styles where it can emulate architectural detailing appropriate to a period house. Wood grain is best reserved for architectural accents and focal points such as wainscots, panel inserts, and fireplace surrounds and mantles.

Don't overdo it: think of these effects as the jewelry that can make an elegant room really shine. Woodgraining a whole room is more likely to be overwhelming than impressive, although in special cases it may be appropriate. You can also use the method shown here to create faux-hardwood floors if you like—just be sure to cover the finish with a few coats of clear floor finish to prevent the effect from wearing off.

Wood graining is an advanced technique that involves using several faux skills to produce one result. Even if you're fairly proficient with more basic techniques, practice this one a few times before you take it to the dining room wall.

➡ **ADVANCED.** Mastering the graining tools takes some practice.

wood grain

Woodgraining uses one of the most specialized tools we'll talk about in this book: the graining comb and the heart grainer. You can buy both tools separately at some home improvement stores, specialty paint stores, or crafts stores; others have both functions combined in one tool. You'll also need a few hot dog rollers, a flogging brush, and conventional painting tools.

PAINTING WITH THE GRAIN

A graining comb or grainer is a rubber comb. Its teeth vary in width from narrow on one end to large on the other. It's used to create a grain pattern that resembles the sap wood, or outer portion of a log or board. The heart grainer, on the other hand, is a quarter-round tool with rubber ribs in concentric rings on its rounded surface. You move it down the surface of your finish with a rocking and dragging motion to create a grain effect that mimics the heartwood, or center of a log or board.

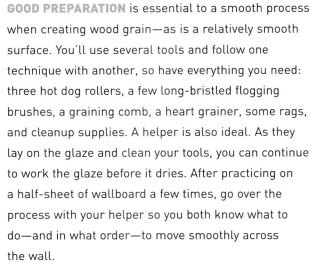

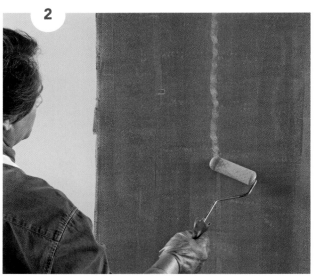

GOOD PREPARATION is essential to a smooth process when creating wood grain—as is a relatively smooth surface. You'll use several tools and follow one technique with another, so have everything you need: three hot dog rollers, a few long-bristled flogging brushes, a graining comb, a heart grainer, some rags, and cleanup supplies. A helper is also ideal. As they lay on the glaze and clean your tools, you can continue to work the glaze before it dries. After practicing on a half-sheet of wallboard a few times, go over the process with your helper so you both know what to do—and in what order—to move smoothly across the wall.

1. **Lay down the background and glaze.** Use the lightest color you can find in the wood as your background color. (Here I'm using a buttercup color I had custom-mixed for a satin finish paint.) Roll the paint on and let it cure overnight. Then choose the next most dominant colors on the sample board and mix those up as glazes—in this case, the colors are burnt sienna and raw umber. The lighter color is usually the heartwood in the middle of the plank, the darker color is the sapwood at the plank's edges. Choose colors that have a fair degree of hue separation between them, or the resulting finish will look homogeneous and muddy in color, rather than variegated like real wood. Mix the glaze and have your partner roll each color glaze on in about a 4-inch vertical band. Use a separate hot dog roller for each glaze, and mix the two colors together where they meet.

2. **Hold a third hot dog roller at an angle** to the wall so only the rounded end touches the wall surface, and use your background color paint to make a highlight line down the center of the lighter section of glaze. This represents the tree's initial growth.

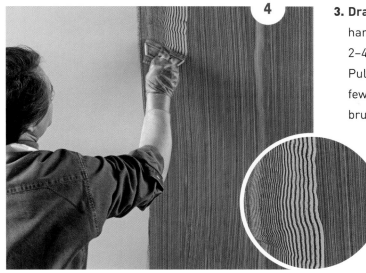

4

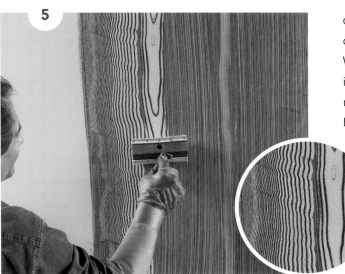

5

3. Drag the surface with a flogging brush. Tip the handle at a slight angle to the wall, so the last 2–4 inches of the bristles contact the wall surface. Pull the brush down the height of the wall. Make a few passes over each wall section, wiggling he brush randomly every so often to imitate grain, which is rarely perfectly straight. Normally you'll create a typical plank width of approximately 4 inches. I'm working on a wider scale here so the effect shows clearly in the photos.

4. Pick up the graining comb. Hold it so the thickest teeth of the comb face toward the "inside" of a plank—in this case, it's to my right. Drag the comb down through the glaze with a steady pressure. Wiggle the comb a bit every now and then to introduce some character into the grain. (I tell my wood grain painting students to drink lot of coffee before class, because the more twitchy your hand movements are, the better!)

5. Pick up your heart grainer. Here comes the fun part! A heart grainer is truly a wizard's wand—a magical tool that quickly creates a finish with all the irregularity of real, center-of-the-tree wood grain with just the flick of a wrist. To use the tool, start at the top of the wall and drag it smoothly and quickly straight down the wall. Overlap the tool slightly with the combed grain you've just applied. And most importantly, ROCK the tool, changing the angle of the handle to the wall in a smooth rocking motion as you drag the tool downward. That's what creates the irregularly spaced grain markings you see here. The "wavelength" of the grain—the distance between the u-shaped grain lines at the center of the drag—is determined by how quickly you rock in relation to how quickly you drag. So

Make a tray trolley

When applying paint or glaze with a roller, it would be helpful if your roller tray full of paint followed you around the room. It can: Buy a round, wood or plastic plant roller, the kind people put under large potted plants that need to be moved often but are too heavy to pick up and carry. Using large spring clamps attach your roller tray to the plant roller and you've got a tray trolley that you can move easily as you paint.

study your sample board and experiment to see how quickly to rock your wrist on the way down. It sounds complicated, but you'll soon find a rhythm that replicates the type of grain you're after.

6. Repeat Step 4. Pick up your graining comb again, and hold it so the wide teeth face the inside of the board—the "heartwood" you've just created with the heart grainer. Again, drag the comb down the wall, overlapping slightly with the lines created by the heart grainer. Now you're creating a mirror image of the grain on the other side of the heartwood. Just like you did on your first pass with the comb, wiggle and twitch every so often to introduce some waviness in the grain. With these three strokes—graining comb, heart grainer, graining comb—you've created the basis for the reproduction of a single board.

7. Start working on your second "board" by flipping your graining comb over so the wide teeth point toward the left again. Make another drag. Follow it with another slightly overlapping pass with the heart grainer, then another slightly overlapping

pass with the graining tool. Continue this pattern, making adjacent vertical passes until you've grained the entire 4×8 section of glazed wall.

8. Create the fine grain. The graining tool and heart grainer make exaggerated, coarse, almost cartoonlike grain lines. These lines reproduce the wood's growth rings, which vary dramatically in color. Now it's time to add the fine grain of the individual wood fibers that you can see when looking closely at a smoothly planed board. This fine grain reduces the wood's contrast, adding dark lines to predominantly light areas, and light lines in predominantly dark areas throughout the board. Fortunately there's another magic tool that quickly adds these lines for you: a flogging brush. Use the brush to "slap" the finish. Flog the wall lightly with the sides of the bristles, which pick up glaze from the dark areas and deposit it in the light areas. Notice the difference in contrast between the "plank" to the left in this photo, and the "plank" that I've been flogging, on the right. The coarse grain is still there, but it's softened by the presence of the fine

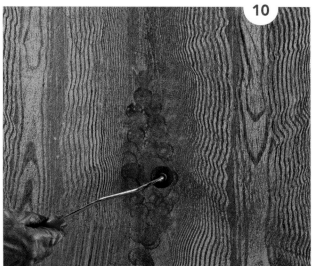

grain introduced by the brush.

9. **Now drag a regular brush** down the wall to create the impression of longer grain fibers. Don't drag straight down, but change your wrist angle every now and then, introducing ripples and cross-grain similar to those you observed in your sample plank.

10. **What "knot" to do.** Even fairly straight-grained wood has a knot or two in it, and adding a few here and there to your "paneling" increases its' realism. Do this randomly: knots that line up or repeat regularly won't look realistic. Make knots by dipping the end of a hot dog roller in the darkest color glaze you're using and tapping it off on the rake of the glazing tray. Apply the end of the roller to the wall and twist it to form a small, burl-like impression. Then flog over it with the flogging brush to blend it in with the grain around it.

The real thing

Grain painting works best if you use it to reproduce the look of an actual board. Here's how:

Choose a board. Visit a lumberyard, home center, or wood specialty store and pick out a board you like. Look for interesting grain structure, good color, and a species that's normally used as a display wood. Coarse-grained woods, such as pine, oak, and cedar, are easiest to reproduce; extremely fine-grained woods, such as cherry and maple, can be more difficult.

Analyze the color. Generally I try to isolate three colors in my wood sample. I use the lightest color for the background, or highlight color, and pick out two of the darker colors as well. Then I match each color to an exact tone on my color wheel. I have paint mixed to match the highlight, and mix glaze to match the other colors.

Note the grain pattern. Take a close look at your board, which should be as wide and as long as the effect you want to create. Check the width of the growth rings that determine the grain, and how often the heart grain repeats. Replicate these dimensions when creating your effect.

rock on!

When most people say they have "sheet rock" walls, carrara marble is not what they mean. But with a little finesse, that's what you can have.

marble

MARBLE IS ONE OF THE MOST EXOTIC MATERIALS used to embellish architecture—and among the most difficult to work with. But you can recreate the look of polished stone and have it be amazingly convincing. In fact, faux marble is in some ways even more impressive than the real thing, because your eye and skill can replicate a material that takes nature eons of time, heat, and pressure to produce.

Marble is another technique you don't want to overdo. A little goes a long way. Use it sparingly and appropriately to add accent to architecture, such as on a fireplace surround, a wainscot, or as a decorative inset panel. That degree of understatement is called STYLE, and bespeaks of a reserve that's always in good taste.

There are many different types of marble, and each have their own character. In addition, each piece of marble is unique. So visit a cut stone supplier and look at their samples. Choose a piece that has a look you'd like to reproduce, and buy as large a chunk as practical. I particularly like the softly veined, almost mystical look of Carrara marble, and I prefer basing my design on an actual stone at least 18 inches square.

> **ADVANCED.** Combines lots of tools and techniques.

The tools and materials used to create a marble finish are surprisingly common. However, unlike simpler effects applied with one or two tools, a marble finish requires quite a few. This makes keeping track of and cleaning the tools a bit of a challenge. This is also a technique where having a helper makes all the difference. While you add the positive effects, he or she can apply the clear glaze and keep your tools clean and organized.

WHAT YOU'LL NEED

Here are a few items to have on hand: sea sponges, hair clips, glazes pre-mixed in colors taken from your stone sample, glazing trays, a large soft-bristled brush, conventional roller frames and rollers, clear glaze, and a No. 2 artist's brush. Don't necessarily limit yourself to these, however: Take a good hard look at your sample slab and ask yourself what tools might help you recreate it.

153

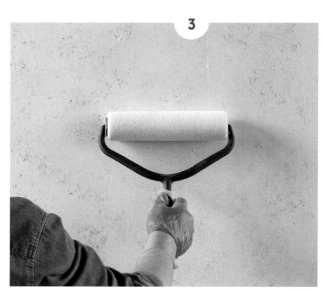

about generating a marble finish is that you can "scale up" the effect. I visually enlarge the pattern of an 18-inch square chunk of rock to cover about a 4×4-foot section of wall. The result looks just fine, and using an actual stone as a model helps create

Marble is, for the most part, a positive effect—you're adding glaze to a base coat in a very controlled way, rather than removing it. Positive techniques are less forgiving of errors than negative ones, so practice, confidence, and experience are especially useful in their execution.

a realistic look. Have satin paint matched to the stone's lightest, most predominant color. Roll this paint onto the wall and let it cure overnight.

1. **Sponge on drifts of the darkest color** in your stone sample. Most marble is quarried so the grain runs on the diagonal to resist cracking. This diagonal grain produces drifts, the darker hues that show as a "Milky Way" effect in the rock. To create a convincing marble look, replicate the angle as well as the color and character of the drift. Grab a sea sponge with a hair clip, dip the sponge in the glaze, tap it off on the rake of the glaze pan, and "pounce" the sponge lightly on the wall surface.

2. **Soften the drifts** by picking up a dry softening brush and pouncing the bristles on the sponged color. The bristles will absorb and redistribute some of the black glaze, softening the effect.

3. **Further soften the effect** by rolling on clear glaze in 4×4-foot sections of the wall. Maintain a wet edge as you roll.

4. While the glaze is still wet, brush lightly over the vein in random directions. The clear glaze reactivates the black glaze so it will flow, and brushing it while wet helps to feather it in further, creating a wispy look characteristic of carrara marble.

5. Add a second glaze color. In my stone sample, the second most common color was a mustard shade, and that's what I'm working with here. Pounce it on with a clean, damp sea sponge, following the pattern in your sample stone. Continue to observe and follow the oblique angle of the stone's grain.

6. Soften the drifts by picking up a dry softening brush and pouncing the bristles on the sponged color, just as you did with the black drift. The bristles will absorb and redistribute some of the black glaze, softening the effect.

7. Reglaze. Before the second color glaze dries, roll on another coat of clear glaze. Your roller will pull up some of the colored glaze and reapply it elsewhere on the surface, softening the area. This combination of techniques is called "stacking and blending:" stacking, because you're applying colors one on top of the other, and blending, because the colors mix somewhat in the process. You add colors one by one, glazing with a clear coat between colors. The more you stack and blend, the deeper and richer the result. Just as you see through multiple semitransparent layers of crystal in real marble, you can look down through multiple layers of semitransparent finish. As with other faux effects, though, remember to step back from the wall, look at the overall result, and know when to stop before the surface becomes too homogeneous.

8. Add veining. Once you're satisfied that you've replicated the soft drifts of color that permeate a typical slab of marble, it's time to move onto the narrower, more definite lines called veins. First, let your last coat of glaze dry for at least 20 minutes. Now take a No. 2 artist's brush and saturate it with glaze that replicates the color of the stone's veining—in this case, black. Hold the brush by the end of the handle, so that any arm movements you make are amplified by the length of the handle, and so that you can see the line you're creating easily. With the brush at a slight angle to the wall, drag, wiggle, and twist the brush to create jagged, irregular lines like those on your sample. The veins should resemble cracks and fractures in the rock, and should vary randomly in length and size.

9. Add more veins of the same and different colors, crossing the lines and traversing the field at angles suggested by your sample. Here I'm adding some lines representing veins of a different color mineral with burnt sienna glaze.

10. Soften the veins. Dip a sea sponge in clear glaze and tap off the excess on the rake of the glaze pan. Then use the sponge to "pounce" some of the veins, forming a halo effect that adds to the vein's realism.

the perfect glaze container

Especially when you're using several different glaze colors and applying them at different times to create a single finish, it's handy to have a glaze container that's easy to use. Make several out of clean, empty dish soap bottles into which you dispense your glazes after you mix them. The bottles are clear, so you can see what color glaze they contain, they're airtight, so the glaze won't dry out, and the squirt top allows you to dispense just the amount you need into a tray or plastic plate pallate. Much better than working with cans!

BURNT SIENNA 124

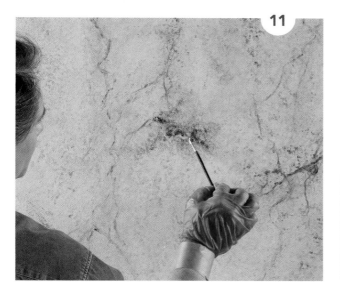

11. Create a character mark. These marks occur where darker minerals flow and diffuse through the broken rock in a random pattern. If the drifts resemble the Milky Way, character marks resemble distant galaxies: clusters of tiny specs and lines viewed indistinctly, as from a distance. You can use a combination of tools to form these marks: sponges, softening brushes, and artist's brushes. Simply brush in a little white glaze to add contrast to the darker colors. Go ahead and experiment, then take a close look at your sample slab, and see what works for you.

12. Voila! With some practice you can achieve effects that are so realistic that if you held up your sample slab in front of your finish as I am here, it would blend into the painted background. Pretty cool, huh?

lots of choices!

Now that you've learned how to execute so many finishes, what's right for you? **Consider your home's period**—when it was built. Try to choose materials that would have been available to the original builder. Executing a marble effect in a rustic log cabin, to choose an extreme example, would look entirely inappropriate—no matter how beautiful the effect.

Consider your home's architectural style. Many finishes shown in this book are notable for reproducing the colors, textures, and materials of a particular style or region. If your home is designed in a French provincial style, for example, a textured effect might complement its architecture nicely.

Consider your furnishings and accessories. Faux finishes are great at creating a backdrop. Choose one that complements the color, style, and design of your furnishings, artwork, and other accessories.

Consider the "mood" of the room. Are you seeking to create a place of energy, or serenity? Coziness or drama? Choose an effect that supports your desired mood.

dramatic diamonds

Diamonds add a vibrant, theatrical look that no other effect can duplicate. Your choice of color, contrast, and scale customize the look.

DIAMONDS CAN BE A WALL'S BEST FRIEND. I like them because their diagonal lines add an unconventional dimension and energy to a room. Appropriately scaled, they can make a room appear both wider and taller.

You can use high-contrast diamonds, such as a black-and-white pattern, to create drama and whimsy. Subtle, tone-on-tone diamonds can add pattern and elegance—in a dining room, for instance. Sometimes I'll cover an entire focal point wall with the shapes. Other times I'll use diamonds on just part of the wall—below the chair rail, as a wainscot treatment, for example.

As with stripes, painting diamonds is a no-brainer: You just roll on the glaze. All the work is in the preparation. You'll need a calculator to determine the scale of the pattern for the room's size. You'll also want to stock up on masking materials and hobby-knife blades to ensure a precise, worry-free job.

One of the great advantages of creating a diamond pattern with paint rather than with preprinted wallcovering materials is you can scale the pattern to fit your room exactly. This gives you more flexibility and doesn't confine you to a predetermined dimension right off the printing press. There's nothing as pleasing as diamonds executed on a wall so their points terminate precisely at a wall's four edges. The symmetry "hits the spot," complementing the architecture of your room better than a generic decorating product.

ADVANCED. As with stripes, the challenge is in the layout.

diamonds

The first tool you need is a calculator to help you lay out a grid that perfectly matches your architecture. You can use an estimater's model to calculate feet and inches, but I find it easier to use a regular calculator and calculate all measurements in inches. You'll also need a chalk line and white chalk pencil to mark the layout on the wall.

MASKED FOR DRAMA

Once you lay out the pattern, the quality of the effect will depend largely on your masking skills. Buy a lot of masking tape—now is not the time to be chintzy. Don't use the stuff left over from an old paint job. More than likely, the adhesive dried out and won't provide a good, paint-proof seal. You'll also need a razor-sharp utility or hobby knife and some "press and seal" plastic wrap. The stuff sticks to just about anything, and works well to mask areas too large for tape. Finally, grab a paint roller, tray, and other conventional paint tools.

TOOL PROFILE

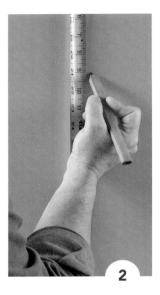

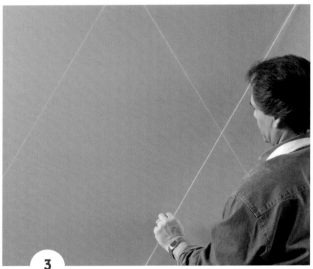

LAY OUT YOUR PATTERN

- Determine the width of your diamonds. First, measure the length of your wall. Lets say it's 144 inches. Since you want the diamonds to fit the space precisely, try to find a number that divides into 144 equally, and gives you the approximate scale of the diamonds you want. You can divide 144 by 36 to get four vertical rows of 36-inch-wide diamonds to fill the wall exactly. Other options include 36 four-inch-wide diamonds or eight 18-inch-wide diamonds. Choose the scale you think looks best.

- Determine the height of your diamonds. A standard 8-foot wall is 96 inches tall, so you could have four courses (horizontal rows) of 24-inch diamonds or three courses of 32-inch diamonds, and so on. Keep in mind that diamonds look best when their width is fairly close to their height.

- Draw the result on graph paper, along with any architectural features (doors, windows, fireplaces, and built-ins) and major pieces of artwork and furnishings that will adorn the wall.

- If the scale looks awkward, redivide the wall measurements and redraw different scale diamonds until you're pleased with the layout.

1. **Mark the width of the diamonds on the wall** using a tape measure and chalk pencil.

2. **Mark the height of the diamonds** the same way.

3. **Snap a chalk line** that connects the points you've marked on the wall. Lightly mark the diamond shapes you'll paint with a chalk pencil "X."

4. **Tape along both sides of the chalk line.** Although you'll cut away half the tape you apply, you can tape a long line much faster and more accurately than you can a series of short lines, so you save time and get better results by "wasting" some tape on this step.

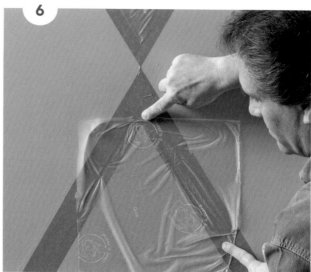

5. Cut away the inside layer of tape on every diamond that you've marked with an "X" in Step 3. To do this, simply make neat diagonal cuts at the corners of each marked diamond as shown, then peel the tape off.

6. Mask off the interior of each unmarked diamond with a special plastic wrap called "Press 'n Seal." Press the wrap firmly against the masking tape for a good seal, then cut off any excess with a sharp utility knife. For areas larger than a single width of plastic wrap, overlap the wrap approximately 1 inch, and press-seal the seam.

multicolor diamonds

Every once in a while, someone will ask me if it is possible to use more than one color when executing a diamond finish, and if so, when to pull the masking tape. The answer is yes, you can, but you still need to pull the tape 60 minutes after the first finish dries. That means you'll need to remask the entire wall before you add the second color coat. I do this regularly, but I'm used to masking and can do it precisely and fairly quickly. For someone who hasn't worked a lot with masking tape, the thought of remasking an entire wall is pretty daunting. That's probably a good thing, because unless you're incredibly skilled at applying tape, you're likely to be unable to precisely match your first application. The result: Each diamond will have two edges, giving the whole effect a slightly fuzzy, out-of-register look that seriously detracts from the results. That's why I usually recommend avoiding double-taping and multiple colors, and encourage adding effects, such as dragging, that result in a more layered look without requiring remasking.

7. Paint the unmasked diamonds with a hot dog roller. You can use a conventional roller, but it won't save much time, and it wastes a lot of paint. I prefer to use the smaller, lighter, more maneuverable hot dog rollers even for relatively large-scale diamonds such as these.

8. For additional texture, paint about three diamonds, then stop and comb the surface with a brush or other combing tool (see combing, page 107). This isn't an essential step but a variation that helps soften the effect, adding a subtle variegation to the surface, and providing a nice contrast to the sharp points, crisp lines, and rhythmic dimensions of the diamonds.

9. Pull the masking materials—tape and plastic wrap in one unit—60 minutes after you've applied the finish. Pull the materials straight down, rather than straight out, to minimize stress on the surface.

trash tips

There's lots of stuff that gets thrown away during a faux finishing job, and some of it is pretty messy: roller tray liners, used painting gloves, stirring sticks, cans and lids, paint-encrusted masking tape. This isn't the kind of stuff that an ordinary trash container was made to hold. So do yourself a favor and line every trash receptacle in and around your work area with at least one, and preferably two plastic trashcan liners. That way, the mess will stay in the liner, and you won't have to add "cleaning paint-encrusted wastebaskets" to your cleanup list when the job is done. And empty trash containers frequently as you work—an overfilled container is just asking to topple over, drip, or leak.

RAGGED RAGGED

Our culture doesn't have a large vocabulary for color or visual effects, so its easy to get off on the wrong foot when you use words alone to describe the effect you want—whether it's to your painting contractor or your spouse.

"Just do a rag finish in this room," the client told me, so after agreeing on the color, I did. She hated it, so I painted over it and did it differently. She hated that too.

It didn't take a genius to see we were having a communication problem. Since I'd just worked for two days for nothing, I decided to spend a little time trying to figure out a way to communicate exactly what I was going to do without having to paint the whole room first. I don't mind rejection—I just don't like it to take all day!

The problem is single descriptive word—such as "ragging"—can describe a tremendous variety of finishes. There had to be a better way.

That day, I bought a stack of canvas-covered boards from my local craft store. Now, after discussing a finish with a client, I come back to my studio and execute it on the board. Then I bring the board to our next meeting. If the client likes the finish, I cut the board in half then and there. We both sign each half of the board. The customer keeps on half, I keep the other. If the finish on the wall matches the finish on the board, the customer is obliged to pay for the job. If not, I do it over for free (something, I'll a dd, that I've never had to do.)

That helped a lot, but not enough. People were still surprised by what they ended up with—even though they could see that the finish we executed duplicated the sample on the board exactly. Now I go one step further, encouraging clients to tack the board up on the wall that they want finished, and look at it

several times a day in different light. If they find the effect too dark, to light, too subtle, or too dramatic, we can adjust the shade or tint of the color, and the contrast between highlight and shadow to fine tune the finish to their sensibility, and to the wall's location and lighting.

Still, it can be hard for someone unaccustomed to faux finishing to visualize the finished effect as it looks on an entire wall. So we still have to resort to the sample boards every once in a while to show someone we did create exactly the finish they'd specified.

Lesson learned: Don't assume you can visualize the look of a finish from a simple description—or even from a small sample. Practice on a large span of wall in your basement or garage first, so you know what the effect looks like when writ large on a wall—before you attack your living room.

touchable texture

Dimensional stenciling combines visual texture with physical texture, adding a high-low effect wherever it's applied.

DIMENSIONAL STENCILING combines a visual technique with a physical one to create a character that paint alone simply can't achieve. This effect is useful when you want to catch the eye and draw attention to a particular area, not an entire room. I like to use a dimensional stencil as a border around the top of a room, where it almost looks like a gesso applique.

I also use dimensional stencils in combination with other effects. For instance, I'll create a leather background, then punctuate it with a raised stenciling of buttons painted with a metallic finish such as copper or chrome. Used in this way the stenciling is a nice relief (literally!) to flat paint, because it offers physical highlights and shadow as well as visual contrast. Think of this technque as jewelry: It's the bit that adds the bling.

Don't try this on a ceiling, folks. I did once. The job ended up looking great, but I decided then and there that no amount of money was enough to make me willing to endure the mess and discomfort of working overhead with this technique.

ADVANCED. Involves both color and texture.

stenciling

Choose a stencil design among the variety available in quality painting, crafts, decorating, and home improvement stores. Buy four identical stencils, which are made of laser-cut acetate. You'll need that many to keep your project moving along smoothly.

STENCIL AND COMPANY

The stencil itself is only one of the things you'll need. While you're at it, purchase some repositionable spray contact adhesive, sometimes known as stencil adhesive. Don't use regular contact cement: You'll never get the stencil off the wall! You'll also need a bucket of standard, premixed drywall compound, which you should stir well before using. Finally, get out your drywall knife, tape measure, white chalk pencil, glaze mixed to your color preference, and a good-sized, good-quality paintbrush.

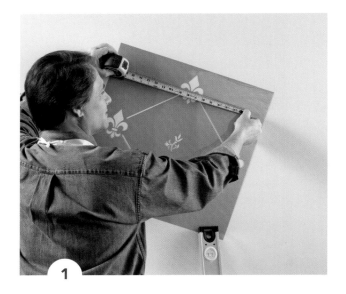

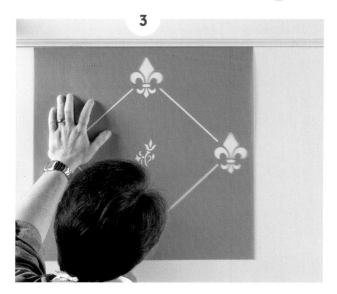

WHAT A RELIEF!

The whole point of this effect is to create a pattern of raised drywall compound that adds a textural element to the stencil design. As with any geometric pattern, layout is critical. To begin, choose a color with a satin or eggshell finish to paint the wall.

1. **Measure the design.** Here I've chosen a fleur-de-lis stencil, and, as with any pattern, it's essential to know the precise repeat. One option to determine this is to try to align the stencils with vertical marks, spaced the width of the stencil itself, along the wall. This can be very hard to line up though. The better choice is to pick an exact point on the stencil's design, and scribe a vertical line that runs exactly through that point. Here I'm measuring the distance from the point of one fleur-de-lis to another.

2. **Scribe a vertical line.** Once you determine how far apart the "register points" are, scribe vertical lines down the wall at that interval with a white chalk pencil. Don't use a regular pencil—the lines will permanently mark and smear the wall. Chalk pencil erases easily, and disappears when glazed over. That makes it perfect for this purpose.

3. **Apply the stencil to the wall.** Lay the stencil down, wall-side up, on an old towel or drop cloth and spray the stencil with repositionable contact adhesive. This gum-based adhesive is not affected by water or wallboard compound, and does not create a permanent bond. Those qualities allow you to remove the stencil and reposition it elsewhere on the wall for the next application of compound. To ensure even coverage, spray on one light coat using horizontal strokes, turn the stencil 90 degrees, and spray on another light coat. (I like to use a spray can trigger, available at any paint store, to ease this job.) Align the stencil with your register marks and press it to the wall.

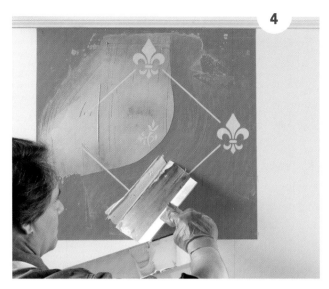

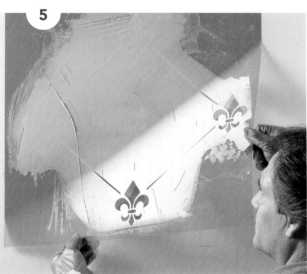

4. Trowel on the mud. Mix your drywall compound thoroughly, using a mixing attachment, available at any hardware or home improvement store, and an electric drill. Any lumps or inconsistencies in the compound will show up as flaws on your wall. Don't try to apply the compound directly from the heavy, awkward bucket it comes in. Transfer some into a smooth-sided mudding tray and carry that with you as you go. You'll work much faster and more comfortably, and because most of the mud remains in its sealed container, you don't risk drying out the unused compound. Apply the compound so that it fills all voids in the stencil. How thick to apply it depends on the effect you want. For a refined, polished look, you want a smooth, even application. For a more rustic look, slather it on more thickly and unevenly.

5. Pull the stencil off the wall after the compound has solidified, but notcompletely dried, approximately an hour after application. Pull from the bottom of the stencil up at a shallow angle, so most of the compound stays on the stencil.

tricks of the trade

These three tips can save you a lot of mess and hassle:
Keep a can of vegetable oil spray and a spare, clean foam roller cover on hand. Lightly spray the top surface of the stencil with vegetable oil. This will make it a bit slick, helping you to press it to the wall with the roller cover without wrinkling or moving the stencil.

Pull the stencil off the wall about an hour after applying the compound. The compound will stay on the stencil, and because it's not fully cured, will wash off easily. If you wait much longer to pull the stencil, the compound will dry on the stencil, and crack and flake off as you remove the plastic, making a mess of your floor. The dried pieces that remain on the stencil are also difficult to clean off.

Use a large, shallow, disposable aluminum foil roasting pan with a snap-on lid half-filled with water and a scrub sponge to clean stencils. Use another roasting pan with some lacquer thinner in it to clean the stencil when it becomes gummy with adhesive. Snap the cover on this pan when you're not cleaning to reduce fumes.

6. Skip a space, then stencil again. Let the stencil pattern dry. Move the stencil over, skipping one application of the design, and begin troweling on the compound again. Don't stencil adjacent to a stencil you've just removed—doing so disturbs the fresh compound. That's why I like to buy multiple stencils; then I can do an entire horizontal row, called a course, at a time. Work in a checkerboard pattern: Stencil in the first course spaces 1, 3, and 5. After an hour, pull those stencils and move down one row, stenciling spaces 2, 4, and 6, so the newly-applied stencils never disturb the drying compound.

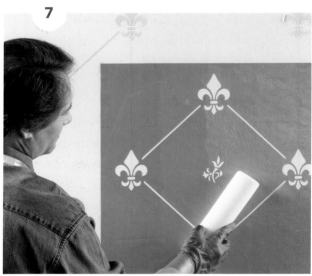

7. Stenciling the second course. Use a foam roller as a smoothing tool to apply a stencil in the second course to the wall. When you finish applying the checkerboard pattern to the wall, quit for the day to let all the applications dry. The following day, fill in the blanks on the checkerboard. Use approximately half the wallboard compound on the second day; the stencil will overlap the two patterns on either side.

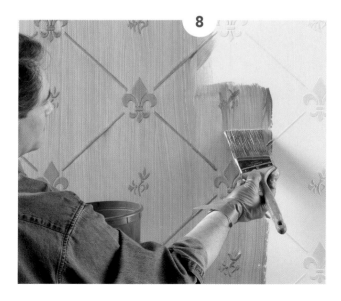

8. Glaze the wall. When preparing your color glaze, mix it with an equal part clear glaze to produce a more translucent mixture. Paint it on the wall with even, vertical strokes. You may be tempted to use a roller here, but the striations created by a brushed finish are part of the handcrafted look, so resist the urge to speed up the job. As you apply the glaze, you'll notice that the textured elements appear darker than the background. That's because the raw, unprimed joint compound absorbs more glaze than the satin-finished paint on the rest of the wall. The result visually enhances the effect's texture.

9. **Continue to brush the surface.** Make sure to cover all the stenciled areas. Since the glaze is very thin, it will run easily, and you may need to brush out some drips.

10. **As the glaze starts to gel,** drag down the surface with the brush. You can also dab the surface randomly, creating irregularities in the finish that suggest age.

11. **For a variation,** further distress the effect by sanding the wall lightly after the glaze has dried 36 to 48 hours. Use 100-grit sandpaper or a sanding screen on a drywall sander to lightly go over the finish. The sandpaper will abrade some of the stenciled texture—and the glaze it has absorbed—off the wall, giving it the weathered look of timeworn plaster.

12. **Further touch up your distressing** with a hand sanding block, also with 100-grit sandpaper on it. Once the finish looks just the way you like it, you can either leave it as is, or apply a clear glaze over the whole wall. The clear glaze will "freeze" the effect, preventing it from degrading further. Leaving it unglazed will allow the wall to continue to age with time.

don't answer the phone

It seems silly, but some people will be right in the middle of a complex faux finishing project, with glaze or drywall compound drying on the wall as they work, and tools in hand. Then the phone will ring—and they answer it! By the time they get back to work, their rhythm is off, the materials have dried out, and the effect is ruined. So, don't answer the phone! Or at the very least, turn the volume on your answering machine way up and ignore any call that's not an emergency.

index

index (continued)

metric conversions

U.S. UNITS TO METRIC EQUIVALENTS			METRIC UNITS TO U.S. EQUIVALENTS		
To Convert From	**Multiply By**	**To Get**	**To Convert From**	**Multiply By**	**To Get**
Inches	25.4	Millimeters	Millimeters	0.0394	Inches
Inches	2.54	Centimeters	Centimeters	0.3937	Inches
Feet	30.48	Centimeters	Centimeters	0.0328	Feet
Feet	0.3048	Meters	Meters	3.2808	Feet
Yards	0.9144	Meters	Meters	1.0936	Yards
Miles	1.6093	Kilometers	Kilometers	0.6214	Miles
Square inches	6.4516	Square centimeters	Square centimeters	0.1550	Square inches
Square feet	0.0929	Square meters	Square meters	10.764	Square feet
Square yards	0.8361	Square meters	Square meters	1.1960	Square yards
Acres	0.4047	Hectares	Hectares	2.4711	Acres
Square miles	2.5899	Square kilometers	Square kilometers	0.3861	Square miles
Cubic inches	16.387	Cubic centimeters	Cubic centimeters	0.0610	Cubic inches
Cubic feet	0.0283	Cubic meters	Cubic meters	35.315	Cubic feet
Cubic feet	28.316	Liters	Liters	0.0353	Cubic feet
Cubic yards	0.7646	Cubic meters	Cubic meters	1.3079	Cubic yards
Cubic yards	764.55	Liters	Liters	0.0013	Cubic yards
Fluid ounces	29.574	Milliliters	Milliliters	0.0338	Fluid ounces
Quarts	0.9464	Liters	Liters	1.0567	Quarts
Gallons	3.7854	Liters	Liters	0.2642	Gallons
Drams	1.7718	Grams	Grams	0.5644	Drams
Ounces	28.350	Grams	Grams	0.0353	Ounces
Pounds	0.4536	Kilograms	Kilograms	2.2046	Pounds

To convert from degrees Fahrenheit (F) to degrees Celsius (C), first subtract 32, then multiply by $\frac{5}{9}$.

To convert from degrees Celsius to degrees Fahrenheit, multiply by $\frac{9}{5}$, then add 32.

notes

notes

notes